Student Activity Workbook

COMPANION TO

Jade

Mosdos Press
CLEVELAND, OHIO

acknowledgments

ISBN 09671009-6-8 Student Activity Workbook
COPYRIGHT © 2004
MOSDOS OHR HATORAH, CLEVELAND, OHIO
All rights reserved. Printed in U.S.A. Fourth Printing.
This publication is protected by copyright and all duplication or reproduction is prohibited. Storage in a retrieval system, or transmission in any form or by any means, electronic, mechanical, photocopying, recording, or otherwise are also prohibited. This copyright will be strictly enforced. For information contact Mosdos Press, 1508 Warrensville Center Road, Cleveland Heights, Ohio 44121.

Mosdos Press Literature

EDITOR-IN-CHIEF
Judith Factor

EXECUTIVE EDITOR
Libby Spero

SENIOR EDITORS
Jill Brotman, Abigail Rozen

COPY EDITOR
Laya Dewick

TEXT AND CURRICULUM ADVISOR
Rabbi Ahron Dovid Goldberg

table of contents

SHORT STORIES

RECOGNIZING PLOT:
- Rikki-tikki-tavi 6
- A Day's Wait 12
- Kid at the Stick 18
- Look Back at the Sea 24

DEFINING CHARACTER:
- Stolen Day 30
- The Strangers That Came to Town 36
- Barnum's First Circus 42
- A Secret for Two 50
- "My Journey Is Still Long" 56

EXPLORING SETTING:
- The Dinner Party 62
- The Third Level 68
- Rip Van Winkle 74
- A Boy and a Man 80
- The Hummingbird That Lived Through Winter 86

UNDERSTANDING THEME:
- The Sparrow 90
- Zoo 96
- The Clearing 102
- Home on the Range 108
- The Sound of Summer Running 114

PULLING IT ALL TOGETHER:
- The Circuit 122
- Home 128
- Child Pioneer 134
- The Runner 140
- After Twenty Years 146

table of contents

NONFICTION

HUMAN INTEREST:
- Cat on the Go 152
- The Night the Bed Fell 158

BIOGRAPHIES AND AUTOBIOGRAPHIES:
- *from* Barrio Boy 162
- Helen Keller 168
- Roberto Clemente: A Bittersweet Memoir 174

HISTORICAL ESSAYS:
- Florence Nightingale 180
- Morning—"The Bird Perched for Flight" 186

ADVENTURE ESSAYS:
- Rattlesnake Hunt 192
- Beneath the Crags of Malpelo Island 198

DRAMA

- Penicillin and Company 204
- Grandpa and the Statue 210

THE NOVEL

The Voyages of Dr. Dolittle
- Part One 216
- Part Two 222
- Part Three 228
- Part Four 234
- Part Five 240
- Part Six 246

Glossary 252

Student Activity Workbook

Mosdos Press
CLEVELAND, OHIO

Rikki-tikki-tavi

VOCABULARY
Activity 1

| cunningly | flinched | gait | mourning | valiant |

1. I am embarrassed to admit that I am afraid of cats. Yesterday, Sally's handsome orange cat approached me and I _____ (drew back, as if from something dangerous).

2. Logically, it doesn't make sense to have such a fear of felines. Why can't I be more _____ (brave)?

3. Part of me feels that a cat thinks very _____ (craftily), but that's ridiculous. A cat is just a cat.

4. I know that when Jennifer's cat died, she was in _____ (a state of grieving over death), almost as if her cat were a person.

5. Sally thinks I'm silly. As we sat at lunch she said, "Susanna, just look how gracefully cats move—look at their _____ (manner of walking, stepping, or running)!"

Name _____

Rikki-tikki-tavi

VOCABULARY

Activity II

Circle the word that is completely *unrelated* to the vocabulary word.

cunningly	flinched	gait	mourning	valiant
cleverly	embraced	walk	grief	courageous
craftily	backed away	sing	lament	stout-hearted
clumsily	retreated	run	celebration	brave
shrewdly	drew back	step	bereavement	cowardly

1. Who might behave **cunningly**?
   _____

2. When would someone **flinch**?
   _____

3. How would you describe a horse's **gait**?
   _____

4. When is a person in **mourning**?
   _____

5. For what type of work or actions must a person be **valiant**?
   _____

Using Your Dictionary

The vocabulary word *mourning* is a noun. The related verb is *mourn*. Using your dictionary, look up the definition of *mourn*, and write it on the line below.

mourn _____

The vocabulary word *cunningly* is an adverb. The related noun is *cunning*. Using your dictionary, look up the definition of *cunning*, and write it on the line below. Make sure you get the definition of the noun and not the adjective!

cunningly _____

Rikki-tikki-tavi

MORE ABOUT THE STORY
Writing Activity

In your textbook on page 16, Question 6 asks you to explain how Kipling arouses sympathy for Nagaina. In fact, our feeling two opposite ways about Nagaina—that she is both good and evil, that she is a threat but that she also deserves mercy and tenderness—shows us how good a writer Rudyard Kipling is. Now it is your turn to be Nagaina. In the first-person voice, using the pronoun *I*, write your feelings as Nagaina, as you plead with Rikki-tikki-tavi for the life of your last egg.

Name _____

Rikki-tikki-tavi

MORE ABOUT THE STORY

Writing Activity

Short Stories ~ (Textbook p. 4)

Rikki-tikki-tavi
GRAPHIC ORGANIZER
Identifying Characters

Complete the pyramid by writing the correct names and descriptions in each square.

THE HERO

Nag
Male Cobra

THE ANTAGONISTS

THE THREE MAIN CHARACTERS

Darzee
Male
Tailorbird

THE FOUR MINOR CHARACTERS

The Veranda

THE FIVE SETTINGS

Short Stories ~ (Textbook p. 4)

Rikki-tikki-tavi

GRAPHIC ORGANIZER
Identifying Characters

Name _____

Reading fiction is one of the most painless ways of picking up all kinds of information. Facts that you might find boring in a textbook are fascinating when they are part of an exciting plot. Think about Rikki-tikki-tavi. Have you noticed how much you have learned about the habits of snakes, mongooses, muskrats, and tailorbirds? Fill in the index cards with facts you have learned about the topic listed on the card.

1. What does a mongoose look like? _____

2. Would the mongoose make a good family pet? Explain. _____

3. What do mongoose eat? _____

4. What are the size, shape, color, and outstanding features of the cobra? _____

5. How are the baby cobra born? About how many are born at a time? _____

6. What is the best way for a mongoose to kill a snake? _____

Short Stories ~ (Textbook p. 4)

A Day's Wait

VOCABULARY
Activity 1

> commenced   flushed   purgatives   varnished
> covey   poised   slithered

1. Robert had never seen anything so remarkable. Like a snake, Harry Houdini _____ (moved or walked with a sliding motion) out of the cabinet while it was underwater, in spite of his being handcuffed!

2. Jane shouted, "I will never take castor oil! I do not want to take any kind of _____ (medicine that cleanses the intestines)! How awful!"

3. As the parade moved down Euclid Boulevard and turned left onto South Taylor Road, the band _____ (began) to play the national anthem. The spectators lining the street joined in and loudly sang "The Star-Spangled Banner."

4. Can you see Willa? There she is, _____ (to be balanced or held in suspension) at the starting line. I just know she is going to win the race.

5. Talking about a _____ (small group of game birds) of partridges is similar to referring to a group of lions as a "pride" or a group of fish as a "school." Did you know that a group of larks is called an "exultation"?

6. This magnificent dining room table dates from the Victorian period. It looks a bit rough, but if it is sanded and _____ (coated with varnish), it will lose its value as an antique.

7. When members of the aristocracy hunted for entertainment, they rode on horses, blew bugles, and sent a pack of dogs after a fox that they _____ (drove out from hiding) from its hiding place. They called it "riding to hounds."

A Day's Wait

VOCABULARY
Activity II

Name _____

Meet Mixed-Up Moby

Mixed-Up Moby often thinks that the definition of a vocabulary word is just the opposite of what it *really* is. Please help Moby out and fill in the blanks below.

1. **Commenced** means ended! It really means _____.

2. When you take a **purgative**, you feel all stuffed up. But a purgative really _____.

3. The carpenter **varnished** the cabinets so that their surface would look dull. Actually, when a surface is varnished it looks _____.

4. A **covey** is a large group of lions. It really means _____.

5. To **slither** is to run like the wind. It really means _____.

6. When the group of men **flushed** the coyote from its burrow, they were helping it hide. No! Flushed means _____.

7. **Poised** is slouching, not ready to do anything. It really means _____.

Unscramble

1. Unscramble each word and fill in the letters on the blanks.

    d**h**ira**v**n**s**e   _ _ _ _ _ _ _ _ _

    shufled   _ _ _ _ _ _ _

    memo**cc**en**d**   _ _ _ _ _ _ _ _ _

    thredlies   _ _ _ _ _ _ _ _ _

    evocy   _ _ _ _ _

    grupevi**t**a   _ _ _ _ _ _ _ _

    de**p**ios   _ _ _ _ _ _

2. Combine all the boldfaced letters and unscramble them into four words that answer the question below.

    What saves nine?

    _ _   _ _ _ _ _ _   _ _   t_ _ _ _

Short Stories ~ (Textbook p. 18)   13

A Day's Wait

MORE ABOUT THE STORY
Writing Activity

> In *A Day's Wait*, the boy is unable to share his feelings and fears with his father. Have you ever had an experience that frightened you, and you found yourself unable to share your feelings with those to whom you are close? Describe your experience, and write what you would have said, if you had been able to do so.

Short Stories ~ (Textbook p. 18)

Name _____

A Day's Wait
MORE ABOUT THE STORY
Writing Activity

Short Stories ~ (Textbook p. 18)   15

A Day's Wait

GRAPHIC ORGANIZER
The Power of Suggestion

"It's like kilometers and miles."

Most of us are very *suggestible*. This means that, like the boy in the story, we react to what we *believe* to be true, as strongly as if it were actually true. The exercise below is a sort of game. Under the section entitled **Kilometers** you will find a list of apparent facts. None of them is really true but, due to lack of information or some misunderstanding, you believe them to be true. Under the column **Miles** write a brief description of how you would react to those "facts."

Kilometers

Miles

Example:

1. You are sitting in math class and feel as though you really understand what the teacher is saying. Your friend whispers to you that she saw your grade on the last exam, and she thinks you failed.

2. Last night you had a sleepover at your best friend's house. Today she leaves school early to go to the doctor. You hear that she has strep throat.

3. The boy you sat next to in class was sent home with lice.

4. On the bus home, the little girl behind you coughed and sneezed on your neck at least ten times.

Example:

1. *You suddenly feel confused by the math and are sure you do not understand anything being taught.*

2. _____

3. _____

4. _____

Short Stories ~ (Textbook p. 18)

Name _____

A Day's Wait
GRAPHIC ORGANIZER
The Power of Suggestion

Kilometers   **Miles**

5. A girl in your class has a new dress. You're not sure whether you like it or not until you hear it was purchased at the fanciest store in town.

5. _____

6. You've heard some boys on the basketball team laughing at how badly you play. You are in the middle of a game and, unexpectedly, the ball is passed to you.

6. _____

7. Your friend offers to lend you his bike. As you get on, he warns, "Be careful, it's very wobbly!"

7. _____

8. You make yourself a glass of cocoa and enjoy its warm, chocolatey taste. Then your mother comes in and says, "By the way, there was some sour milk in the fridge—don't drink it."

8. _____

9. You enjoy playing with your neighbor's dog until the neighbor comes out and says, "I sure hope that flea powder worked."

9. _____

10. The gym teacher tells two new students to run around the track. To the first student he says, "You probably will not be able to run the entire course; no one ever has. But don't worry, if you can run 3/4 of it, we'll be happy." To the second student he says, "This course is a quarter mile shorter than the one we usually ask the students to run. You'll probably finish it with plenty of energy to spare." How do you think each student will do?

10. _____

Short Stories ~ (Textbook p. 18)   17

Kid at the Stick

VOCABULARY
Activity 1

ailerons   bank   bellowed   Mayday   synchronize

1. My dad is a public service pilot for the government. He flies his plane in search and rescue operations, medevac and air ambulance, and gets called on for emergency services like forest fire fighting. Ever since we were little, my sister and I have played pilot games. Always, before we start, we scream, "Let's _____ *(set timepieces or watches to the same time)* our watches!" This makes us feel like it's official and serious.

2. We've learned all the words for parts of the plane from dad. He's even taken us on board and shown us. So don't be surprised if you hear Beth warning me, "It's too soon for you to start a _____ *(a controlled tilt made by a turning plane)* to the right. You'll hit Mt. Wazoo!"

3. "And don't forget," she continues, "you can't bank unless you adjust all your _____ *(moveable surfaces near the trailing edge of aircraft wings, used for banking).*"

4. "Stop _____ing *(roaring like a bull; crying out in a deep, blaring voice)* at me, Beth. You're disturbing my concentration. A pilot on a rescue mission must concentrate!"

5. All of a sudden I see Mt. Wazoo looming ahead of me. "Beth!" I cry. "I'm in trouble. _____ *(an international radiotelephone distress signal used by ships and aircraft)*! I need help, fast!"

Short Stories ~ (Textbook p. 24)

Name _____

Kid at the Stick

VOCABULARY

Activity II

What's Wrong With This Sentence?

Explain what is wrong with the meaning of the sentence on the lines provided.

Example: When we were rocking the baby to sleep, we bellowed a lullaby.
Bellow means to roar like a bull, which would not help lull a baby to sleep.

1. The pilot did not want to bank, so she made certain the **ailerons** were working.
   _____
   _____

2. Douglas insisted that they **synchronize** their watches, since they would be involved in different activities at various times.
   _____
   _____

3. The search and rescue mission went extremely well, because when the pilot had to fly straight, he invariably started another abrupt **bank.**
   _____
   _____

4. We had a flock of lambs that would wake us when they **bellowed** in the early morning hours.
   _____
   _____

5. Things were going really well—this was my first solo flight—and so to reassure my friends on the ground, I said into the speaker, "**Mayday!**"
   _____
   _____

Short Stories ~ (Textbook p. 24)

Kid at the Stick

MORE ABOUT THE STORY
Writing Activity

Have you ever thought what it would be like to fly a plane? Or what it takes to be licensed as a pilot? How *do* people become pilots? What sort of training is involved? What kinds of jobs are available that are *not* part of the airline industry? Here's your chance to track down this information. Go to the library, have the librarian direct you to the right sources, and write a short report describing the training and licensing and the types of jobs available to a licensed pilot.

Name _____

Kid at the Stick

MORE ABOUT THE STORY

Writing Activity

Short Stories ~ (Textbook p. 24)

Kid at the Stick

GRAPHIC ORGANIZER
Creating Suspense

Kid at the Stick is a suspense-packed story about the dangerous landing of a small plane. The story is written in a well-designed format: as the plane *descends*, the tension *mounts*.

If we analyze the story, we can learn how a writer creates tension and suspense. The diagram is designed to point out how, with a few well-chosen words, a writer can create a tremendous sense of anxiety in the reader. The path that starts at the top of the page traces the route of the plane as it slowly descends. The path that starts at the bottom of the page traces the rising suspense in the story. Write the words or phrases that the author uses at each point to create suspense into the boxes on this path.

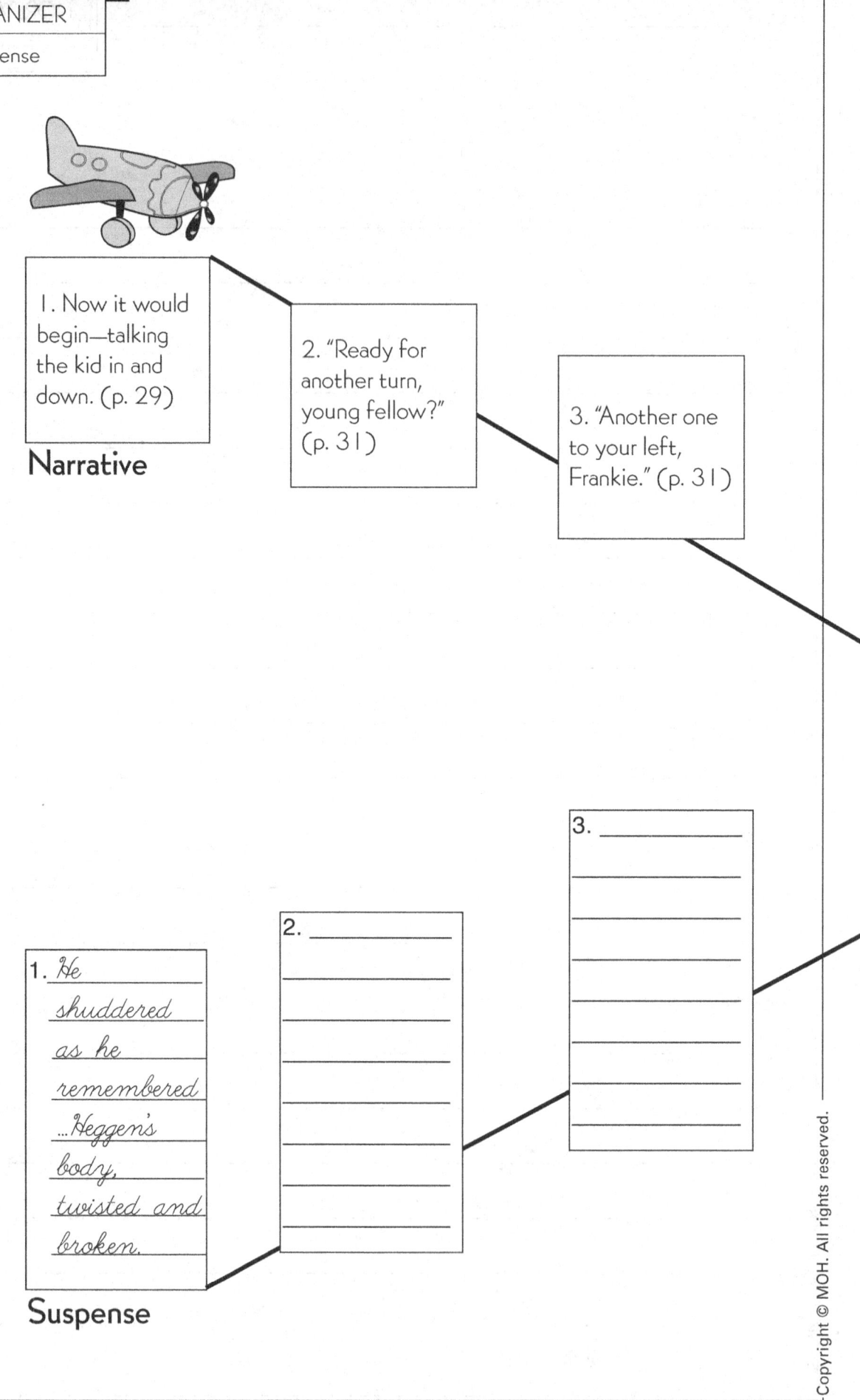

Narrative

1. Now it would begin—talking the kid in and down. (p. 29)

2. "Ready for another turn, young fellow?" (p. 31)

3. "Another one to your left, Frankie." (p. 31)

Suspense

1. He shuddered as he remembered ...Heggen's body, twisted and broken.

2. _____

3. _____

Name _____

Kid at the Stick

GRAPHIC ORGANIZER

Creating Suspense

6. _____

5. _____

4. _____

4. "Now lower your nose." (p. 32)

5. Lower and lower the plane came...It looked professional... (p. 32)

6. He could hear the engine now. Even throttled... (p. 33)

Short Stories ~ (Textbook p. 24)   23

Look Back at the Sea

VOCABULARY
Activity 1

| dunes | horizon | marina | swell |

1. The old man went out in the early morning in his boat, as he had done nearly every day for the past fifty years. His wife had said, "Don't go, Sam. They're forecastin' bad weather. You ain't been feeling right." When he had shrugged, she'd added, "Please don't take chances, Sam." But he'd just answered quietly, "Doris, we be needing the money from today's ketch." He sat now, in his boat, peaceful. How silly folks were, he thought, with all their worryin'. The sea was real calm. Made a fellow feel good. Ain't even the littlest bitty _____ (*a wave, especially when long and unbroken*). But I'm a lucky man, he reminded himself, to have a family that cares for me and looks out for me.

2. At noon, Doris stepped out of the cabin and walked down the pebble path to the water's edge. She moved down the beach slowly, and then just stood with her hands on her hips, looking first to her right, then to her left. She put her hand above her eyes like a visor, to protect them from the sun, and scanned the _____ (*the line that forms the apparent boundary between earth and sky*). True, the waves that broke at her feet were nothin' to speak of. How hard it was not to worry!

3. When three o'clock had come and gone, Doris called to Old Joe. The spaniel raced beside her as she strode, determination in her gait, the three-quarters mile to the ramshackle _____ (*landing pier for docking small boats*) at the center of town—if you could call it a town, she thought.

4. "You seen Sam?" she cried to the men sitting on the dock. "We ain't, Doris," said the tallest fellow, kind of a young man, but real sturdy. "Headed out early this A.M.," she added, as if to explain. A boy about twelve came over and kneeled to pet the spaniel. "Ma'am," he said. "Mebbe you and me could take a look out for the boat, up from them great big _____ (*sand hills formed by the wind near the ocean*). Sam been talkin' about some bluefish he see'd thataways." "Thanks, Sonny," she said softly, gratefully. "'ppreciate the company." And she and the boy and the dog headed for the sand ridge about a mile up the dirt road.

Name _____

Look Back at the Sea

VOCABULARY

Activity 11

Would'a, Could'a, Should'a

In the following exercise, answer the first question with a "yes" or a "no." Then, in a complete sentence or two, explain why you have given this answer.

Example:

Question: Would the **dunes** be a good place for a vegetable garden?

Answer: <u>No. Dunes are sandy hills in the desert or near the ocean. They don't have the soil and water that plants need.</u>

1. Is a **marina** a place to take your car to be fixed?
   _____
   _____

2. When the sun sets, do we see it at the **horizon**?
   _____
   _____

3. If you wanted to ride the waves, would you be hoping for a **swell**?
   _____
   _____

4. If I were looking for a place with hard-packed soil, would I explore the **dunes**?
   _____
   _____

Short Stories ~ (Textbook p. 36)

Look Back at the Sea

MORE ABOUT THE STORY
Writing Activity

Imagine that after her experience that day on the raft, Clara decided that she would never go back to swim or float in the ocean. Read through the first eight paragraphs of the story once more. Now write about the experience Clara would miss, if she never went out again.

Name _____

Look Back at the Sea

MORE ABOUT THE STORY

Writing Activity

Short Stories ~ (Textbook p. 36)

Look Back at the Sea

GRAPHIC ORGANIZER

Skillful Use of Language

Look Back at the Sea follows the classic pattern of most suspense stories. It opens with ordinary protagonists placed in a secure situation. All is well. Something then occurs to alter the secure situation. As the story progresses, the suspense grows. Will the protagonist emerge safely from the danger? At the lowest point in the story, the situation appears hopeless. The story can end in one of two ways. In some stories, the danger proves real and the story ends in disaster. In other stories, the danger is overcome, the hero is comforted, and the situation returns to normal.

The key to each of these steps in the story is language. A good writer will choose words and phrases that create the desired atmosphere. In *Look Back at the Sea*, the language in the opening "secure" section of the story is very different from that used in the "hopeless" section. Below, you will find a jumbled list of phrases from the story. Choose phrases from this list to complete the exercise on the opposite page, placing each phrase in the appropriate column. Try to determine, just from the words, which column each phrase belongs in. You can check to see if you are right by looking back at the story and finding the phrase.

- The smooth, rhythmic rise and fall of the waves.
- "I'm just...glad."
- Her trembling arms.
- The sun was warm on her back.
- Not a dangerous sun.
- The chill of the wind.
- The sound seemed soothing.
- He spoke in the soothing tone people use.
- Her teeth began to chatter.
- She was sleepy, relaxed.
- "It's all right."
- She was overcome with a kind of loneliness.
- Her breathing grew regular.
- She felt as if she had been drawn far away from the normal world.
- The dark choppy water of the sea.
- A spray of cold water slapped across her back.
- Clara would moan.
- A cold fear gripped her.
- She lay with her eyes squeezed shut.
- She no longer yelled or cried.

Short Stories ~ (Textbook p. 36)

Look Back at the Sea

GRAPHIC ORGANIZER

Skillful Use of Language

Name _____

Language of Security

1. _____
2. _____
3. _____
4. _____
5. _____

Language of Fear

1. _____
2. _____
3. _____
4. _____
5. _____
6. _____

Language of Hopelessness

1. _____
2. _____
3. _____
4. _____
5. _____

Language of Comfort

1. _____
2. _____
3. _____
4. _____

Short Stories ~ (Textbook p. 36)

Stolen Day

VOCABULARY — Activity 1

carp   freshet   inflammatory   rheumatism   solemn

1. Do you remember three years ago, when there was a lot of heavy rain? Do you recall the flooding from the _____s *(sudden rises in the level of a stream or flooding caused by heavy rain or rapidly melting snow)* down by the railroad tracks and the old depot? Well, my cousins live on Wicklyffe near Sutton, you know, where the rich folks live. There wasn't any flooding there!

2. "I try not to complain, because there's always someone that has it worse—which is kind of irritating since it feels good to complain. But I tell you, Julie, my joints are just about killing me." Grandma paused and poured the tea. "My _____ *(disease characterized by painful swelling and stiffness in the joints or muscles)* has really taken a turn for the worse." Then she joked, "You'd think it was Tapanuli Fever or the Black Formosa Corruption." I laughed. "Oh Grandma, you must think you're Sherlock Holmes!"

3. Charles cleared his throat and his expression was _____ *(very serious, grave)*. He began his lecture, as he usually did, by summing up the tragic and terrible years that Josef Stalin ruled the Soviet Union. "During the Stalinist period, hundreds of gifted novelists and poets ended their lives in prison cells or labor camps. The work of these writers is largely unknown, and their fate is hardly remembered."

4. Adam Sass has written poetry about various animals, including, of all things, the _____ *(large, freshwater fish)*. He describes this fish as a "fine old shoe of a fish, gape-mouthed, sturdy, and wise." What do you think of that?

Short Stories ~ (Textbook p. 46)

Name _____

Stolen Day

VOCABULARY

Activity II

Word Analogies

In a word analogy, you are given two pairs of words. By figuring out how the words in the first pair are related to each other, you can pick the missing word in the second word pair.

Example 1:   **carp** is to **fish** as **robin** is to
   a. bird   b. song   c. car   d. cat
   Hint: A carp is *a type of fish*. A robin is *a type of bird*.

Example 2:   **ball** is to **round** as **box** is to
   a. circle   b. triangle   **c. square**   d. ball
   Hint: A *ball* is *round*. Which word describes a *box*?

1. **solemn** is to **lighthearted** as **happy** is to
   a. cheerful   b. sad   c. tired   d. gay
   Hint: *Solemn* and *lighthearted* are opposites.

2. **freshet** is to **heavy rain** as **parched land** is to
   a. volcano   b. tornado   c. drought   d. snow
   Hint: A *freshet* is caused by *heavy rain*.

3. **carp** is to **harp** as **button** is to
   a. bows   b. mutton   c. blouse   d. clothing
   Hint: *Carp* and *harp* rhyme.

4. **inflammatory rheumatism** is to the **joints** as a **heart attack** is to
   a. the feet   b. the joints   c. the head   d. the heart
   Hint: *Inflammatory rheumatism* affects the joints.

Short Stories ~ (Textbook p. 46)   31

Stolen Day

MORE ABOUT THE STORY
Writing Activity

Stolen Day by Sherwood Anderson is a funny story about a boy who convinces himself that he has inflammatory rheumatism. But what *is* inflammatory rheumatism?

Diseases often sound mysterious and scary until we have information about them. So, how do people get inflammatory rheumatism? How long does it last? What are the symptoms of the disease? Are there any other types of rheumatism besides inflammatory rheumatism? How does a person with inflammatory rheumatism feel? Is there any way to treat it? Was there any way to treat it in Sherwood Anderson's day?

Conduct your research at the library or from an encyclopedia. Then, write a report that answers one of these questions.

_____
_____
_____
_____
_____
_____
_____
_____

Short Stories ~ (Textbook p. 46)

Name _____

Stolen Day
MORE ABOUT THE STORY
Writing Activity

Stolen Day

GRAPHIC ORGANIZER
Recognizing Rationalization

One interesting and very human trait that the boy in *Stolen Day* displays is one we might call "believing what you want to believe." Instead of basing his beliefs on facts, the boy explains away the facts to suit the idea he has fixed in his mind. For example, when he stops "aching," instead of using this as proof that he is healthy, he decides that this is just what happens to someone with inflammatory rheumatism.

In each of the drawings below, you will find a "fact" that should have told the boy that he was perfectly healthy. In the lines under each drawing, write a phrase or sentence that tells how the boy rationalizes (explains away) each fact.

_____
_____
_____

_____
_____
_____

_____
_____
_____

_____
_____
_____

Short Stories ~ (Textbook p. 46)

Name _____

Stolen Day

GRAPHIC ORGANIZER

Recognizing Rationalization

On the surface, the heroes of *Stolen Day* and *A Day's Wait* appear to be similar. On closer inspection, though, they are quite different. To compare them, complete the chart below.

	A Day's Wait	Stolen Day
1. Is the boy actually sick?		
2. What symptoms does the boy have?		
3. Does the parent take notice of the boy's illness?		
4. What is the boy's reaction to his illness?		
5. When the boy goes to bed, how does he feel?		
6. Does the boy wish for his parent's attention?		
7. What is the weather outside?		
8. Is the boy able to forget about his illness temporarily?		
9. What mistake has the boy made about his illness?		
10. In your opinion, why did the boy make this mistake?		
11. What reaction does the boy have when he is told he is not as sick as he thought?		

Short Stories ~ (Textbook p. 46)

The Strangers That Came to Town

VOCABULARY
Activity 1

acrid	cauterizing	galvanized	obscure	superfluous
animosity	contempt	metamorphosis	sedative	teeming
berated	demeanor	mutely	solace	swathed
canine	elation			

1. Swaddling is an age-old practice for soothing young babies. A baby is swaddled, when it is _____ (wrapped) in cloth so that it cannot easily move its arms or legs.

2. The swaddling is a source of _____ (comfort) to a baby. You might even say that it has a _____ (calming or soothing) effect.

3. In some types of surgery, laser light can be used as a surgical knife. This use of laser light means an incision can be _____ (burned)—and the bleeding stopped—as the incision is made!

4. I thought Anne was not being fair. She _____ (scolded) Mildred for barking at the mailman. Mildred is a smart _____ (dog). Only Mildred knows that the mailman is really an alien. But the next day when the mail came, Mildred just stood _____ (silently), as Anne screamed. She had noticed that the mailman had three eyes and four arms.

5. There are four primary taste sensations: bitter, salty, sour, and sweet. It should be no surprise to you that substances taste bitter, when they are _____ (bitter).

6. That afternoon, Jack's _____ (facial appearance) worried me. He was normally so calm. But now he was angry. I could tell he felt a great deal of _____ (ill-will, dislike) towards the people who had made fun of his son. Why had they behaved that way? Their reasons for being so mean were _____ (unknown). How could they have treated a child with such _____ (scorn)?

7. After the housekeeper had left, Robert refolded the laundry. His efforts at tidying up were _____ (being more than is necessary; excessive). But he was impatient waiting for his guests, and didn't know what to do with himself. His impatience had _____ (motivated) him!

8. The biologists went to the Kalahari Desert to conduct plant and animal research. One day, it rained. Suddenly, it was _____ (falling in torrents, as with rain). It didn't last long, and it ended as abruptly as it began. You cannot imagine the _____ (profound change) the abundance of water created in the desert. You should have seen the _____ (delight) on Jeremy's face as he noted the abundance of new animal life.

Short Stories ~ (Textbook p. 54)

Practice with Vocabulary

In each group below, one word or phrase differs from the other four. Circle it. Use a good dictionary if you are uncertain of the meaning of any of the words.

1. **galvanized**
   - excited
   - motivated
   - stimulated
   - discouraged

2. **sedative**
   - calming
   - upsetting
   - soothing
   - tranquilizing

3. **cauterizing**
   - burning
   - searing
   - watering
   - branding

4. **obscure**
   - unclear
   - cloudy
   - blurry
   - understandable

5. **elation**
   - rejoicing
   - mourning
   - delight
   - happiness

6. **swathed**
   - unclothed
   - wrapped
   - swaddled
   - bundled

7. **contempt**
   - scorn
   - appreciation
   - sneering
   - looking down upon

8. **metamorphosis**
   - transformation
   - profound change
   - unchanging
   - shifting

9. **berated**
   - praised
   - scolded
   - lectured
   - chastised

10. **mute**
    - muffled
    - silent
    - dumb
    - talkative

11. **superfluous**
    - unnecessary
    - necessary
    - needless
    - unessential

12. **demeanor**
    - facial appearance
    - behavior
    - conduct
    - secret

13. **acrid**
    - bitter
    - harshly pungent
    - sharp-tasting
    - sweet

14. **solace**
    - rejection
    - comfort
    - warmth
    - consolation

15. **canine**
    - feline
    - dog
    - puppy
    - man's best friend

16. **animosity**
    - hatred
    - liking
    - loathing
    - dislike

17. **teeming**
    - beaming
    - seeming
    - steaming
    - boy

The Strangers That Came to Town

MORE ABOUT THE STORY
Writing Activity

The Duvitches are immigrants (p. 55). What is an *immigrant*? When did a lot of immigrants come to the United States? How did they get here? Which countries did they come from?

Research these questions and write about the subject on the lines below.

_____
_____
_____
_____
_____
_____
_____
_____
_____
_____
_____
_____
_____
_____
_____
_____
_____
_____
_____
_____

Name _____

The Strangers That Came to Town

MORE ABOUT THE STORY

Writing Activity

Short Stories ~ (Textbook p. 54)

The Strangers That Came to Town

GRAPHIC ORGANIZER
Character Development

In *The Strangers That Came to Town*, there is a clear turning point. Before the fishing trip, the Duvitches behave one way; after the fishing trip the Duvitches behave differently and are perceived differently by the townspeople. In the exercise below, the story is divided into "before" and "after" the fishing trip. Descriptions of the Duvitches and the townspeople's behavior appear in both columns. Some of the descriptions are drawn from the first half of the story, and others from the second half. For every description given, find its parallel in the other half of the story. Write the parallel description down in the opposite section of the chart.

Before the Fishing Trip	After the Fishing Trip
1. The Duvitches were quiet—almost solemn.	1.
2.	2. After a while Mrs. Duvitch found the courage to ask these people into her house.
3. Mrs. Duvitch...was rarely if ever seen in the daytime.	3.

Short Stories ~ (Textbook p. 54)

Name _____

The Strangers That Came to Town

GRAPHIC ORGANIZER

Character Development

Before the Fishing Trip	After the Fishing Trip
4.	4. The children ceased stopping their noses when Mr. Duvitch passed them by.
5. Black hard luck seemed their lot.	5.
6.	6. Even Kasimar began to take on the ways of an American dog, daring to bark and growl on occasion.
7. The young Duvitches...were considered anti-social.	7.
8.	8. They were soon shining in school plays and festivals. Nathan Duvitch could throw and hit a baseball as far as anybody his age in town.

Short Stories ~ (Textbook p. 54)

Barnum's First Circus

VOCABULARY
Activity 1

adroitly	gamboling	laths	uncanny
assented	impudence	pippins	vitality
bland	indefinitely	sorghum molasses	

1. When my sister and I began our archery lessons, I was surprised to see how _____ (*expertly*) she handled a bow and arrow without any previous lessons. Everyone in the family has taken to referring to her as Robin Hood. This is particularly funny because her name actually *is* Robin.

2. The rats could be seen jumping and _____ (*frolicking*) on the mud beach in the moonlight.

3. The quiet was _____ (*mysterious; strange*). She could hear her own breathing, the water dripping from the faucet, the sound of steam in the radiators, but no voices or noises from the building or the street.

4. "So what kind of apples do you like best?" she asked, calling to me from the kitchen. "It really doesn't matter," I said, "especially when it's fall, and they've come right off the tree." I thought about it for a moment. "But I do particularly like _____ (*a variety of apple*) and macouns. Have you ever tried apples dipped in _____ (*sweet syrup from the stalks of cereal grass*)?"

5. The teachers couldn't quite figure Jimmy out. He would answer without being called on, interrupt when others were speaking, and burst noisily into the classroom after recess. Was it _____ (*bold and shameless rudeness*), or just his special brand of _____ (*spunk; energy; exuberant physical or mental vigor*)?

6. Lisa thought that all she would need to do was strip the old wallpaper in the guestroom and put up the new paper she had chosen so carefully. Then, she saw she was going to have to patch the plaster. But when that was done, she realized that she was also going to have to replace a section of _____ (*thin, narrow strips of wood used to make a backing for plaster*) near the closet door. Her mom and dad were coming for a visit on Tuesday. How was she going to finish on time? It seemed like this job was going to go on _____ (*having no fixed or specific limit*).

7. Carla was surprised. Just minutes before, she had asked Richard, the company vice president, to sign off on her contract. Usually he had a million questions. But this time, he had just _____ (*agreed*) with a _____ (*mild; smooth and soothing*) expression, put his signature on the document, and wished her a good day.

Short Stories ~ (Textbook p. 72)

Barnum's First Circus

VOCABULARY — Activity II

Name _____

Crosswords with Vocabulary Words

Fill in the Across and Down answers at the appropriate numbers. Some of the answers are already filled in for you. The clues for those answers are given in bold. (For example, see #3 Down.) If the word to be entered is one of your vocabulary words, the clue will say *vocabulary word*. If the word to be entered is another form of a vocabulary word—for example, *assent* instead of *assented*—the clue will say *from your vocabulary word*.

[Crossword grid with the following filled-in letters:]

- 2 Down / 3 Down area: A S
- 8 Down: I T
- 4 Down: I T L Y
- 12 Down: N T
- 15 Across: A E
- 18: G M
- 14 Across: D N A
- 25 Across: A S T E R S
- 35 Across: R O P E S
- 40 Down: F E E
- 42: M
- 43: G E E
- 45: U
- 49: S O
- 50: O O R
- 54: D
- 56 Across: L E E
- 57: V E E
- 59: G
- 60/61: D T
- 62/63: A T
- 65: K
- 66: P T

Short Stories ~ (Textbook p. 72)   43

Barnum's First Circus

VOCABULARY
Vocabulary II

Across

2. The opposite of *difficult*
5. To weep heavily with little gasps
7. To go to see someone at their house
9. "Pick one ____ the other!" my mother said.
11. Having no fixed limit *(vocabulary word)*
13. The opposite of *yes*
14. The abbreviation for deoxyribonucleic acid, which carries genetic material
15. The past tense of *eat*
16. "Pick up the phone, and listen for the _____ tone."
18. Skips, dances, frolics *(from your vocabulary word)*
21. A youngster is called a _____
22. To agree *(from your vocabulary word)*
25. Flowers with white, pink, or blue rays around a yellow center
27. "Eighth, ninth, _____, eleventh"
28. Mysterious, weird *(vocabulary word)*
31. Where you sit and work in school
33. The opposite of *Ma*
34. The opposite of *A.M.*
35. Strong, thick cords; what children use for jumping
39. The opposite of *on*
41. "One, two, _____"
42. To invent in your mind
45. Bold and shameless rudeness *(vocabulary word)*
47. "If you have a question, you should _____."
49. The opposite of *start*
50. 1
51. The opposite of *odd*
53. A person who digs up coal for a living
54. This animal barks!
56. Confederate Civil War General Robert E. ____
57. The letter of the alphabet between U and W
59. A word that means *pleased*, and rhymes with the word *sad*
62. A fold in a skirt
64. Plural of important human organ; the name of a card game
65. "If you want something to eat, just _____."
66. The abbreviation for part-time or platinum

Short Stories ~ (Textbook p. 72)

Name _____

Barnum's First Circus

VOCABULARY

Activity II

Down

1. To bend your head in a short, quick downward movement
2. The abbreviation for <u>e</u>ast-<u>s</u>outh<u>e</u>ast
3. **To be ill**
4. **A pig pen; also, an infection on the eyelid**
5. A slow-moving mollusk that lives inside a coiled shell (plural)
6. "Ring the ____!"
7. Spunk; energy *(vocabulary word)*
8. **A single or particular thing: "I have fifty _____s on my shopping list."**
9. The opposite of *off*
10. To propel a boat: "____, ____, ____ your boat, gently down the stream!"
11. A subcontinent in southeast Asia, formerly a British colony; its capital is New Delhi.
12. **To pester; also, an old horse**
17. The abbreviation for <u>ad</u>vertisement<u>s</u>
19. Smooth and soothing; mild; non-irritating *(vocabulary word)*
20. Thin, narrow strips of wood *(vocabulary word)*
21. Felines; "It's raining ____ and dogs!"
23. **The abbreviation for <u>et</u>cetera**
24. Light brown color
26. The stalk of a plant that supports a leaf or flower
28. The opposite of *lower*
29. What your parents choose to call you after you are born
30. Expert *(from your vocabulary word)*
32. What is left after a fire goes out
36. A variety of apple *(vocabulary word)*
37. **A large, flightless Australian bird that looks like an ostrich**
38. The opposite of *happy*
39. "_____ upon a time..."; half of twice
40. **What a doctor, for example, charges for a service; rhymes with *bee***
43. **A male name; he was King of England during the Revolutionary War**
44. A place that provides food and lodging for travelers; a small hotel
46. The opposite of *pop*; short for mother
47. Everything or everyone
48. The opposite of *give away*
49. **The present tense of *snuck***
52. Short for *evenings*; the opposite of *morns*
54. **Abbreviation for the insecticide <u>d</u>ichloro-<u>d</u>iphenyl-<u>t</u>richloroethane**
55. The opposite of *stop*
58. **The Latin word for *and***
60. What you lose when you stand up; also, a ____top computer
61. What we call it when people create paintings
63. The abbreviation for <u>L</u>os <u>A</u>ngeles

Short Stories ~ (Textbook p. 72) 45

Barnum's First Circus

MORE ABOUT THE STORY
Writing Activity

In *Barnum's First Circus*, Phineas puts together an entertaining show for the townsfolk. The main feature of the show is a three-eyed calf. In the circuses he (and others) created when he was older, the "sideshow" was very popular. On display in the sideshow were people and animals considered to be "freaks," because they were born physically different from most people: They might be very tall, very short, very fat, very tiny.

The physical deformities of the stars of the sideshow were the result of disease or genetic disorder. What do you think about the idea of sideshows, or freak shows, in which people are put on display to satisfy the curiosity of others? Write an opinion piece of several paragraphs.

Name _____

Barnum's First Circus

MORE ABOUT THE STORY
Writing Activity

Short Stories ~ (Textbook p. 72)

Barnum's First Circus

GRAPHIC ORGANIZER
Using Language Effectively

Much of the reason P. T. Barnum could awe and astound people was that the people of his generation had so little knowledge of the world. A snake, a talking bird, a jumping bean—all were fascinating and exotic to the simple countryfolk. Just imagine what they would have thought of some of our modern-day inventions!

As you can see from the story, Phineas Barnum had a way with words. He could make even an ordinary object sound mysterious and exciting—how much more so, something that truly was extraordinary! In each of the circus tents below, an object is pictured. If you were P. T. Barnum standing in front of the tent holding this object, how would you describe it? What would you say to entice the people to buy a ticket to view it?

The Amazing Telephone

Come One! Come All _____
_____
_____
_____
_____

The Unbelievable Blender

Come One! Come All _____
_____
_____
_____
_____

The Secretive Slinky

Come One! Come All _____
_____
_____
_____
_____
_____

Name _____

Barnum's First Circus

GRAPHIC ORGANIZER

Using Language Effectively

The Magical Lightbeam

Come One! Come All _____
_____
_____
_____
_____
_____

The Roaring Cannibal

Come One! Come All _____
_____
_____
_____
_____
_____

The Moving Machine

Come One! Come All _____
_____
_____
_____
_____
_____
_____
_____

The Echo Machine

Come One! Come All _____
_____
_____
_____
_____
_____

The Cyclone

Come One! Come All _____
_____
_____
_____
_____
_____

Short Stories ~ (Textbook p. 72)

A Secret for Two

VOCABULARY
Activity 1

| cataract | cul-de-sac | pension | sheen | stalk |

1. My father has had difficulty seeing for some time now. On Tuesday, he had _____ (an opaque or cloudy condition on the lens of the eye that impairs vision) surgery. He hated being in the hospital, and he says he looks like a pirate with the patch on his eye, but we are all excited about his vision improving.

2. You may think it odd that anyone would even think about this, but Jane has always admired the gait of horses. We were walking through the Boston Public Gardens one day last week. When she saw the mounted police, she cried out, "Just look at those proud beasts! Just look at how those horses _____ (walk in a slow, stiff manner) down the garden paths!" Well, I had to agree with her. They certainly were dignified and handsome.

3. Silas removed the old cloth sack from the desk drawer. His hands trembled as he shook out the remaining coins to count them. He still had to buy food for the week, tobacco for his pipe, and some bones for Charlie. Charlie looked up and woofed. Silas shook his head in worry. "Well, old friend, there's not much left from the monthly _____ (a payment received periodically by a retired person)." He patted Charlie's head to comfort them both. Would they make it through ten days until the next check came in the mail?

4. Jeremy decided that if he was going to buy a house, he needed to think about what mattered to him about where he lived. A fireplace and a grape arbor would be nice. He definitely wanted a lot of trees. He was a writer, and every writer needs privacy and quiet. Jeremy also needed a lot of space, or he felt crowded. It came to him that if he could find an old Victorian in good condition, on a _____ (a street that is closed at one end) in the city, or on a country road, it would be the perfect place to write his next book.

5. George ran into Arthur as he raced up the stairs. Arthur was gasping for breath. George noticed there was an odd _____ (luster) to his face. "Hey, Artie, what's up?" Arthur collapsed on the top step and put his head in his hands. George repeated his question, and Arthur burst into sobs.

Name _____

A Secret for Two

VOCABULARY

Activity II

Where Do Words Come From?

Etymology teaches us about the origins of words. Learning word roots is an important part of learning language. Learning word roots also helps you expand your vocabulary.

For this exercise, you need a dictionary that gives the origin of the word, in addition to the definition. Your job is to look up four vocabulary words, and write down the information that tells where the word came from.

When the dictionary indicates which language a word comes from, it may use the sign < instead of the word *from*. The language the word comes from is always abbreviated: **L** for Latin, **Gk** for Greek, **F** for French, **E** for English, **G** for German, and so forth. Many dictionaries have a list of these abbreviations. If you see an **M** or an **O** with one of these other letters, it stands for Middle or Old. An **H** stands for High. **OHG** means Old High German. These modifiers tell us how long ago the word was used.

Let's take one of your vocabulary words, *cataract.* For *cataract*, the dictionary says

Latin cataracta waterfall, portcullis, from Greek kataraktes, from katarassein to

dash down, from kata- + arassein to strike, dash.

This means that the word entered English from Latin and meant waterfall or portcullis. A portcullis is the grate that goes up and down at the entry to a castle. The Latin word came originally from Greek. *Cataract* comes from a Greek prefix *kata* + a base word *arassein*, which meant to strike or to dash. Now you try your hand at it. If you need, ask your teacher for help. This takes practice!

1. *cul-de-sac* comes from _____
2. *pension* comes from _____
3. *sheen* comes from _____
4. *stalk* comes from _____

Most dictionaries give the word root information only for the base word. For example, *inhumane* has no information about the origin of the word, but its opposite, *humane*, which is the base word, has information about the source of the word. Sometimes it is hard to figure out from the original word why a word means what it does today.

Short Stories ~ (Textbook p. 82)   51

A Secret for Two

MORE ABOUT THE STORY
Writing Activity

Take one morning, one afternoon, or even a full day, and remind yourself to look very carefully at the places, people, and things that you see. If you can, think of yourself as a character in a story. Give that character a name. In the evening, write several paragraphs about what your character would have missed, if he or she could not see.

Short Stories ~ (Textbook p. 82)

Name _____

A Secret for Two

MORE ABOUT THE STORY

Writing Activity

A Secret for Two

GRAPHIC ORGANIZER

Elements of Writing Prose

The short story, *A Secret for Two*, is easily divided into three sections. Each section has an opening and a closing line. The first section establishes the loving relationship between Pierre and Joseph, the second section describes how Pierre and Joseph grow old together, and the third section tells us about Pierre and Joseph's last days together. The basic outline of the story is filled out and enlivened by much detail and description. The finishing touch of the story is the "hiding" of clues about the surprise ending in each of the three sections.

On the next page, a chart has been divided into three sections, one for each section of the story. All the elements of the story—opening and closing lines of each section, details, descriptions, and foreshadowing (clues about the ending)—are listed in a jumble on this page. To complete the chart on the opposite page, select the appropriate phrases from this page and write them on the lines provided.

- And I cannot see Joseph again
- So it went for years—always the same
- The horse would smile at Pierre
- Montreal is a very large city
- Tears streaming down his cheeks
- You know, I think those two share a secret
- The horse's head would drop and he would walk very wearily to his stall
- The softness of the horse's neck
- The horse...was a large white horse
- Pierre's huge walrus mustache was pure white now
- He would walk very wearily to his stall
- Pierre and Joseph grew old together
- Then one morning Jacques had dreadful news
- Joseph didn't lift his knees so high or raise his head quite as much
- It was a cold morning and still pitch-dark
- It was a secret, I think, just between those two
- A kind horse, a gentle and faithful horse
- Why, a blind man could handle my route

Short Stories ~ (Textbook p. 82)

Name _____

A Secret for Two
GRAPHIC ORGANIZER
Elements of Writing Prose

Section One	Section Two	Section Three
Opening Line	**Opening Line**	**Opening Line**
Details and Descriptions	**Details and Descriptions**	**Details and Descriptions**
1. 2. 3. 4.	1. 2. 3. 4.	1. 2. 3. 4.
Foreshadowing	**Foreshadowing**	**Foreshadowing**
Closing Line	**Closing Line**	**Closing Line**

Short Stories ~ (Textbook p. 82)   55

"My Journey Is Still Long"

VOCABULARY
Activity 1

despise   superior

1. Look, there is just no question about it! There is simply nothing more to say. It is clear that my sneakers are _____ *(of a higher quality)* to yours. Sorry. But hey—you won the race. So what's the big deal?

2. John's uncle was like a father to him when his own dad was serving in the armed forces in Iraq. John had quite a temper, more so when his dad was far away. His uncle often said that when a person gets *that* angry, when you feel as though you *hate* someone else, it is as if that other person owns you. John thought a lot about this. He described to his uncle how a certain person at school was always taunting him. "I'm really thinking about what you told me, Uncle Bill," he said. "I'm working hard not to _____ *(regard with contempt)* him!" Uncle Bill nodded wisely and sympathetically.

Name _____

"My Journey Is Still Long"

VOCABULARY

Activity II

Using a Thesaurus and Finding Synonyms

Look up each of your vocabulary words in a thesaurus, and find six synonyms for each.

1. despise

   _____
   _____
   _____
   _____
   _____
   _____

2. superior

   _____
   _____
   _____
   _____
   _____
   _____

Short Stories ~ (Textbook p. 90)

"My Journey Is Still Long"

MORE ABOUT THE STORY
Writing Activity

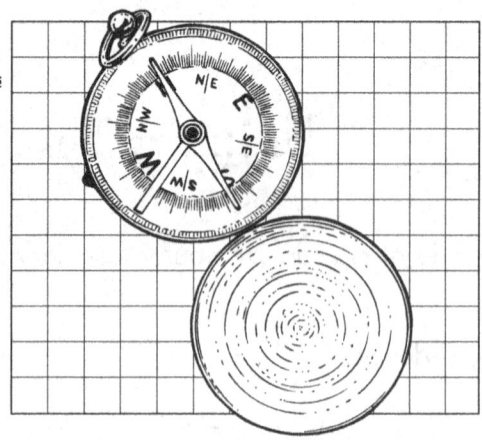

How far can you walk? You are going to go on a journey, with pad and pencil. With your parents' help (using the odometer in their automobile, perhaps), determine a route that you can safely walk that is one or two miles long. Then, with a classmate who has the same assignment, you will make your journey. If it is cold, make sure that you are properly dressed. You need not suffer as Kofi Akakpo did, to complete this exercise! During your walk you will make five stops. At each stop, you and your classmate will sit down on the curb or on a neighbor's stoop, and write about this part of your walking tour. Write about how you feel, the things that you see, and where you are, in each of your entries. The title of your diary is *My Journey Is Still Long*.

Name _____

"My Journey Is Still Long"

MORE ABOUT THE STORY

Writing Activity

Short Stories ~ (Textbook p. 90)

"My Journey Is Still Long"

GRAPHIC ORGANIZER
Concretizing Plot

Charles traveled through three continents. He started in Africa, crossed over to Europe, and finally reached Asia. On this page there is a map that shows the countries Charles visited. There are letters and circled numbers on the map. The letters represent names of countries and the circled numbers represent names of cities. On the page opposite this one there are two lists: one, of letters, the second, of numbers. On the line next to each letter, write the name of the country it represents, and on the line next to each number, write the name of the city it represents. Then, take a pencil and trace Charles' route from Accra to Ankara.

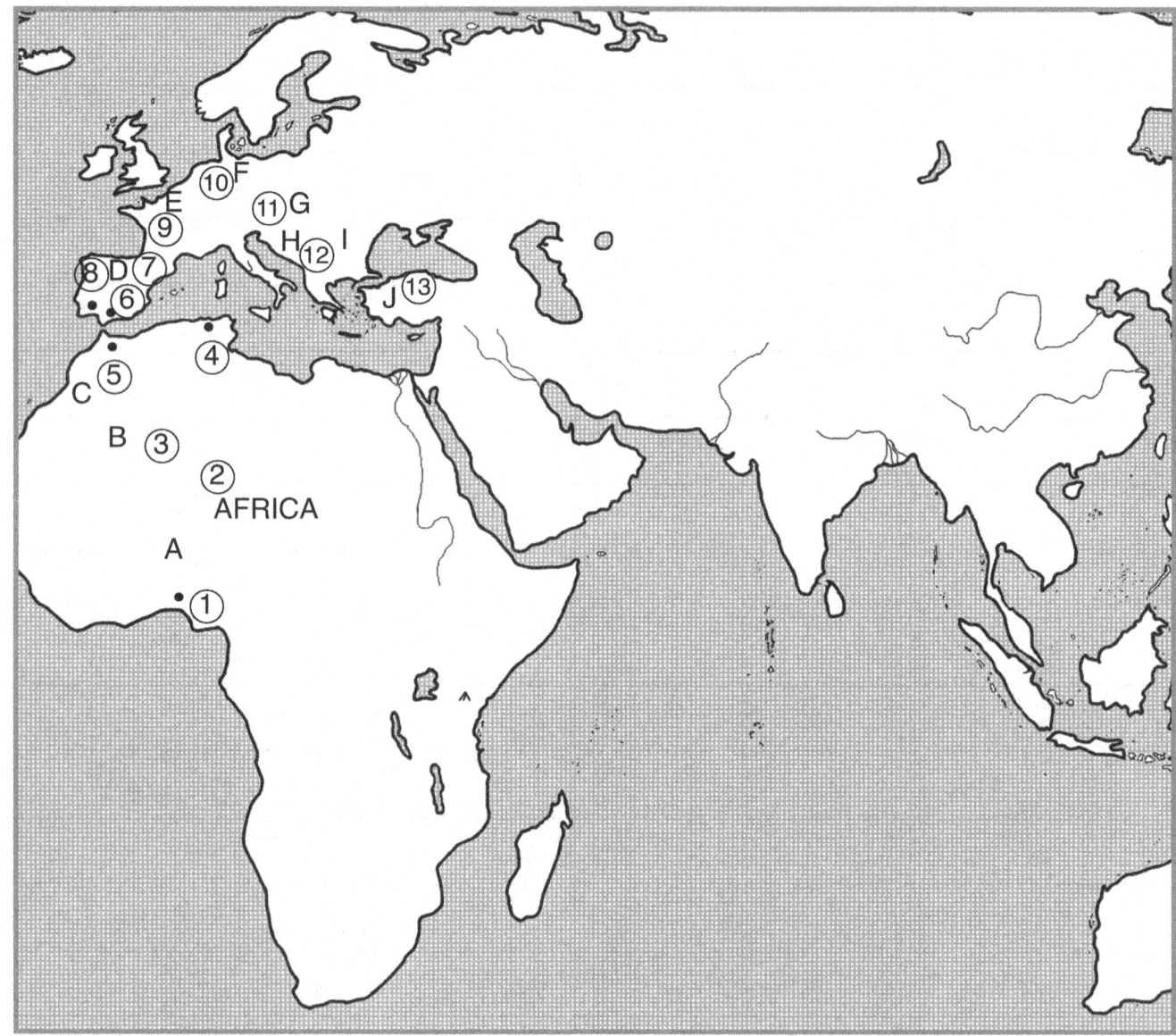

Short Stories ~ (Textbook p. 90)

Name _____

"My Journey Is Still Long"
GRAPHIC ORGANIZER
Concretizing Plot

A. _____
B. _____
C. _____
D. _____
E. _____
F. _____
G. _____
H. _____
I. _____
J. _____

1. _____
2. _____
3. _____
4. _____
5. _____
6. _____
7. _____
8. _____
9. _____
10. _____
11. _____
12. _____
13. _____

ANSWERS: Morocco, Tangier, Bonn, Algiers, Madrid, Sofia
Ghana, Accra, Bulgaria, Yugoslavia, In Salah, Agadès, Seville, Algeciras, Paris, Zagreb
Ankara, France, Germany, Turkey, Algeria, Spain

Short Stories ~ (Textbook p. 90)

The Dinner Party

VOCABULARY
Activity 1

attaché   naturalist   rafters   rupees   veranda

1. *A Shipment of Mute Fate* is a play about a _____ *(person who studies natural science)* who brings a poisonous snake on board a ship. Oddly, he seems to know very little about snakes, and he is convinced that the snake is out to get him. He is not what you'd call an expert in his field. But the play is very entertaining anyway.

2. Grace always brings back different kinds of money when she travels abroad. My son collects "dollar" bills from all over the world, and he always looks forward to her visits when she returns from her travels. She recently came back from visiting India. She stopped by on Sunday, and gave him an envelope containing fifty Indian _____ *(currency of India)*. Little David is only five, and is convinced that now we are very rich.

3. They vacationed at a cottage in Vermont. It was very relaxing in the country. At night they made a fire in the enormous hearth, which was a great comfort. It never became stuffy or smoky, because there was no ceiling—the _____ *(beams of the ceiling)* were exposed in every room.

4. My roommate's mother is a cultural _____ *(a person who is on the staff of an ambassador or diplomat)* at the U.S. Embassy in Turkey. It is unusual for a woman to have such a job in that country, but she speaks eleven languages and her family is very well-connected with Turkish officials.

5. We spend a lot of time on the _____ *(open porch, extending along one or more sides of a building at ground level)*, when the weather is warm. I love to see my grandmother in the large, white wicker rocker. Sometimes, I still sit on her lap, and she sings me a lullaby. I wish she could always baby me.

Short Stories ~ (Textbook p. 100)

Name _____

The Dinner Party

VOCABULARY

Activity 11

Which Word Does Not Belong?

Cross out the word that does not belong with the others.

1. attaché
   professor
   diplomat
   ambassador

2. naturalist
   biologist
   zoologist
   artist

3. rafters
   floorboards
   beams
   roof

4. rupees
   rubbish
   dollars
   currency

5. veranda
   porch
   basement
   deck

Short Stories ~ (Textbook p. 100)

The Dinner Party

MORE ABOUT THE STORY
Writing Activity

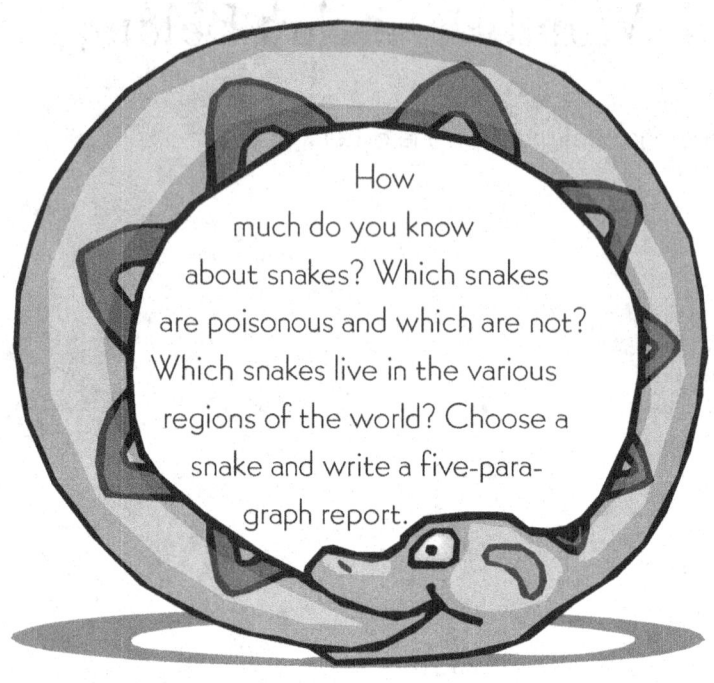

How much do you know about snakes? Which snakes are poisonous and which are not? Which snakes live in the various regions of the world? Choose a snake and write a five-paragraph report.

Name _____

The Dinner Party

MORE ABOUT THE STORY

Writing Activity

Short Stories ~ (Textbook p. 100)

The Dinner Party

GRAPHIC ORGANIZER
From Story to Play

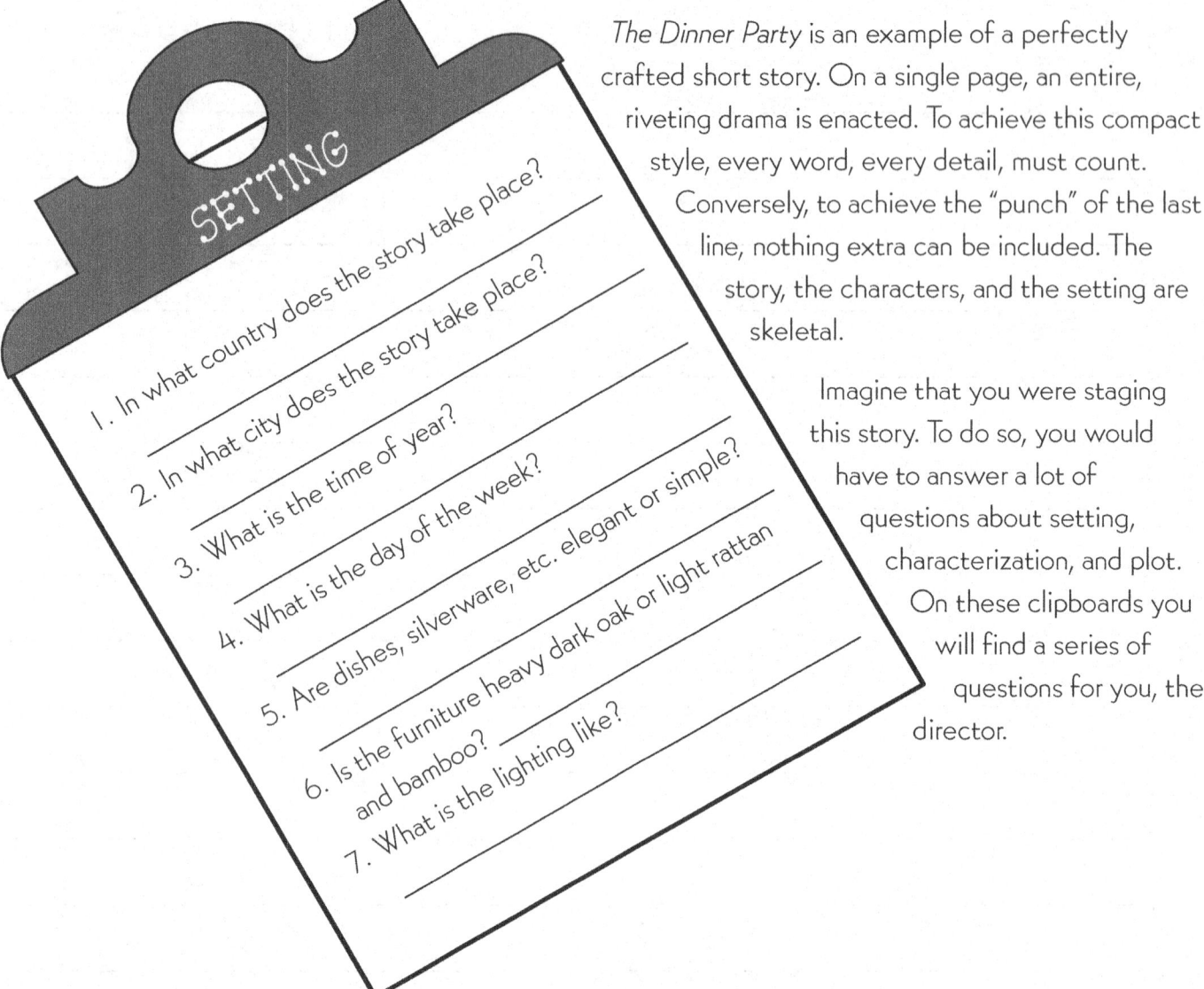

SETTING

1. In what country does the story take place? _____
2. In what city does the story take place? _____
3. What is the time of year? _____
4. What is the day of the week? _____
5. Are dishes, silverware, etc. elegant or simple? _____
6. Is the furniture heavy dark oak or light rattan and bamboo? _____
7. What is the lighting like? _____

The Dinner Party is an example of a perfectly crafted short story. On a single page, an entire, riveting drama is enacted. To achieve this compact style, every word, every detail, must count. Conversely, to achieve the "punch" of the last line, nothing extra can be included. The story, the characters, and the setting are skeletal.

Imagine that you were staging this story. To do so, you would have to answer a lot of questions about setting, characterization, and plot. On these clipboards you will find a series of questions for you, the director.

When you have completed all three clipboards, answer these questions.

Now, go back and count the number of answers that were found in the story. How many were there? _____

Next, count the number of answers you found by inference in the story. There were _____.

Finally, count the number of answers that you had to make up. _____

Short Stories ~ (Textbook p. 100)

The Dinner Party

GRAPHIC ORGANIZER

From Story to Play

Name _____

PLOT

1. What is the significance of milk in a bowl? _____

2. How can that information be conveyed to the audience? _____

3. How should the American show the audience that he knows something is amiss? _____

4. What becomes of the cobra after it is out of the room? _____

CHARACTERIZATION

1. What is the name of the colonial official? Of his wife? Of the American? Of the young girl? Of the colonel? _____

2. Are there others present? If so, how many? _____

3. What does the hostess look like—fair or dark? Fat or thin? Young or old? _____

4. How many women are among the guests? _____

5. How old is the American? _____

6. What type of accent does the American have? _____

Short Stories ~ (Textbook p. 100)

The Third Level

VOCABULARY
Activity 1

corridor currency gabardine premium refuge

1. On November 4, 1992, the United States Congress and the State of Hawaii created the Hawaiian Islands Humpback Whale National Marine Sanctuary. The warm, shallow waters of the Hawaiian Islands are one of the world's most important North Pacific humpback whale habitats. Reports from whalers document the appearance of these majestic giants in Hawaii in the 1840s. Scientists estimate that two-thirds of the entire North Pacific humpback whale population (approximately 4,000-5,000 whales) migrate to Hawaiian waters to have their babies. Whales are mammals and give birth to live young. They nurse their babies and are very protective of them. This sanctuary will provide a _____ *(safe haven; shelter)* essential to the survival of this species.

2. Greta stepped out into the _____ *(long passageway or hallway)* and walked with soft steps down the staircase. Where could she be going so late at night? Should I call to her?

3. Aunt Bee said that _____ *(a durable fabric)* could really be quite elegant, especially in the hands of French clothing designers. Those of us who did not agree, simply remained silent. "Of course," she added, "it's not easy to get French clothes during wartime." I heard someone whisper irritably in the back of the room, "Well, now that we're at war, don't expect *me* to pay a _____ *(an extra amount charged in addition to the usual price)* for gabardine!"

4. The Universal _____ *(Money)* Converter® is a very popular tool that enables us to convert an amount of money from one nation into the money of another nation.

Short Stories ~ (Textbook p. 104)

Name _____

The Third Level

VOCABULARY

Activity II

More Word Analogies

1. **refuge** is to **safe haven**, as **shelter** is to
   a. sanctuary b. house c. garage d. fire station

2. **gabardine** is to **cloth** as **piano** is to
   a. durable b. music c. musical instrument d. symphony

3. **currency** is to **U.S. dollars** as **literature** is to
   a. reading b. fiction c. mathematics d. clothing

4. **premium** is to **extra** as **discount** is to
   a. less b. the same c. more d. money

5. **corridor** is to **rooms** as **highway** is to
   a. animals b. cars c. trees d. cities and towns

Short Stories ~ (Textbook p. 104)

The Third Level

MORE ABOUT THE STORY
Writing Activity

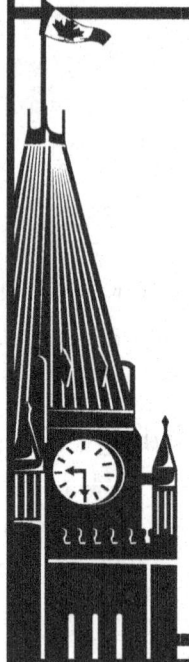

Have you ever wanted to travel back in time? Think about it. Pick a country. Pick a city or town. Pick a century. Read about it. Now, in several paragraphs, talk about what you've learned. Tell your reader what life was like in those days. What kind of houses did people live in? What kind of clothes did they wear? What did they do for work? What kind of medical care did they have, if any? The world of the past that you bring to life can be pleasant or tough.

_____
_____
_____
_____
_____
_____
_____
_____
_____
_____
_____
_____

Short Stories ~ (Textbook p. 104)

Name _____

The Third Level

MORE ABOUT THE STORY

Writing Activity

Short Stories ~ (Textbook p. 104)

The Third Level

GRAPHIC ORGANIZER
Critical Reading

Some folks'r always wishin' they was somewheres else. Take this feller, Sam. Why, he came from another time, another place. An' ah reckon that's where he belongs. But, no, he wants ter be here, in Galesburg, 1895. He likes the "atmosphere" he says. But ah think he's in fer some big surprises.

We think so, too! Describe some of the surprises in store for someone from the 21st century who has gone back in time to the 1890s.

1. It is summertime in New York City and the temperature has hit 95. *Sam turns his air conditioner to high.*	1. It is summertime in Galesburg and it is 95 in the shade. *Sam fans himself and sweats.*
2. Every Sunday Sam washes his pride and joy, a new sports car.	2. Every Sunday, _____
3. Sam enjoys hearing classical music on his CD player.	3. Sam enjoys the music _____
4. Sam's married daughter lives in Florida. He flies down there every winter for a two-week stay.	4. Sam's married daughter lives in Florida. To visit her, he _____
5. Sam sometimes gets a bad case of strep throat in the winter. This calls for _____	5. Unfortunately, Sam catches strep throat in Galesburg. The doctor tells him _____
6. Except during power failures, Sam's apartment is toasty warm all winter long.	6. During the cold Galesburg winters, _____

Short Stories ~ (Textbook p. 104)

The Third Level

GRAPHIC ORGANIZER

Critical Reading

Name _____

On the other hand, Sam may be in for some very pleasant surprises, as well.

1. In the 21st century, Sam takes a subway and a bus to his office, where he works from 9 to 5 every day.	1. In 1895, _____ _____ _____.
2. Sam cannot stand the way people blare their radios in the streets near his home.	2. In Galesburg, 1895, _____ _____ _____.
3. Threats of war and terrorism frighten Sam. The world seems a very small and dangerous place.	3. In 1895, the world _____ _____ _____.
4. Between his job, the news, the computer, the traffic, and the general atmosphere in the city, Sam feels he is under a lot of stress.	4. In Galesburg, 1895, Sam feels _____ _____ _____.

Well—you've heard a bit about each era. Which would you choose, if you could? Why?

_____
_____
_____
_____
_____

Short Stories ~ (Textbook p. 104) 73

Rip Van Winkle

VOCABULARY
Activity 1

chivalrous   keener   martial   obliging   wistfully
incomprehensible   majestic   melancholy   pliant

1. "I do not know how you could have forgotten the meeting!" my boss shouted. "It is simply _____ (not possible to understand)!" I agreed with her. What had I been thinking? There I was, hard at work on my computer at home, when the bigwigs were meeting to discuss the future of the company. How would I ever make up for it?

2. The dog lay on the rug, _____ (feeling sad)—you could just tell by his sad eyes—and Susanna prayed once again that Mary Beth would return *soon* from Indonesia. Sam was Mary Beth's eight-year-old mutt, and he needed Mary Beth to pet him, to sleep with him on the huge oak bed, and to shout "Good old boy," whenever he fetched a stick or a ball. Susanna loved the _____ (regal) beast, but, no doubt about it, he had bonded with Mary Beth and could not be happy without her.

3. Looking up from his reading, Richard told his friend, Galahad, that all of the old scrolls said that _____ (gallant) behavior was part of the _____ (military; related to war) arts. Of course, he added, "It would be easier to be nice, if we weren't suffering under all of that unbearable armor!"

4. Richard stood up and proceeded to trip over Galahad's sword. He lifted it and said, "Don't mind if I move this out of the way, do you?" Then he felt the blade and asked, "How come the edge of your sword's so much _____ (sharper; having a finer edge or point) than mine?" Galahad looked at his friend and just smiled. Richard knew that Galahad was going to be the better soldier and looked at him _____ (wishfully; with longing).

5. Jim's cousin worried that people would think Jim was a wimp. Jim was always so _____ (ready to do favors). Ralph didn't want to hurt Jim's feelings. So he just said to him, "Hey, man, people are gonna think to themselves that you're just so _____ (easily bent; flexible). Yeah, that's just the word they're gonna use. I worry they won't give you enough respect." Jim just laughed at that. "Pliant? I bet they never even heard of that word!"

74   Short Stories ~ (Textbook p. 114)

Name _____

Rip Van Winkle

VOCABULARY

Activity 11

Opposites

Which word means the opposite? Draw a line from each of the vocabulary words to the word or phrase in the second column that has the opposite meaning.

1. incomprehensible   lowly; humble

2. pliant   uncooperative

3. keener   inflexible

4. majestic   peaceful

5. chivalrous   understandable

6. melancholy   duller; blunter

7. martial   discourteous

8. obliging   joyful

Short Stories ~ (Textbook p. 114)

Rip Van Winkle

MORE ABOUT THE STORY
Writing Activity

In your lifetime, what physical changes have been made to the town or city where you live? Perhaps a forest has been cut down for a new mall. Perhaps older theaters have been turned into stores. Perhaps a park has been created or a new highway has been put through. Can you recall the way it was before the changes were made? In several paragraphs, describe your city, town, or neighborhood the way it was before, the way it is now, and whether the changes made were for the good, for the worse, or both.

Name _____

Rip Van Winkle

MORE ABOUT THE STORY

Writing Activity

Short Stories ~ (Textbook p. 114)

Rip Van Winkle

GRAPHIC ORGANIZER
Transitory vs. Timeless

Rip Van Winkle is a story about time and change. But it is also a story about timelessness. The interweaving of the timeless and the transitory (changing) form a beautiful pattern in the story.

In the following exercise, you will find two books. In the first, there are quotations about details that changed while Rip Van Winkle slept. In the second book, there are quotations about details that did *not* change, even with the passage of time. To complete the chart in each book, follow the instructions on the next page.

Transitory

1. There were some of the houses of the original settlers...built of small yellow bricks...having latticed windows and gabled fronts....

2. His wife kept continually dinning in his ears about his idleness, his carelessness, and the ruin he was bringing on his family.

3. Rip's sole domestic adherent was his dog Wolf, who was as much henpecked as his master.

4. For a long while he used to console himself, when driven from home, by frequenting a kind of perpetual club...on a bench before a small inn.

5. ...designated by a portrait of His Majesty George the Third...

6. Derrick Van Bummel, the schoolmaster, a dapper, learned little man...

1. *He found the house gone to decay— the roof fallen in, the windows shattered, and doors off the hinges.*

2.

3.

4.

5.

6.

Short Stories ~ (Textbook p. 114)

Name _____

Rip Van Winkle

GRAPHIC ORGANIZER

Transitory vs. Timeless

Transitory

Find phrases or sentences in the second half of the story that describe how the character or setting in the first half of the story has **changed**. Place the quotation from the second half of the story on the line (with the same number) in the lower half of the hourglass.

Timeless

Find phrases or sentences in the *first* half of the story that indicate that these characters or elements of setting remain **unchanged**.

Timeless

1. There stood the Catskill Mountains—there ran the silver Hudson at a distance—there was every hill and dale precisely as it had always been.

2. Rip Van Winkle preferred making friends among the rising generation, with whom he soon grew into great favor.

3. He took his place once more on the bench at the inn door...

4. As to Rip's son and heir...he...showed an hereditary disposition to attend to anything else but his business.

5. Whenever her name was mentioned, however, he shook his head, shrugged his shoulders and cast up his eyes.

1. *Whoever has made a voyage up the Hudson must remember the Catskill Mountains.*

2. _____

3. _____

4. _____

5. _____

Short Stories ~ (Textbook p. 114)   79

A Boy and a Man

VOCABULARY
Activity 1

| bulged | glacier | imbecile | prone | reconnoiter |
| crevasse | gradually | jutting | pummeled | taut |

1. _____ (large masses of ice and snow) are a fascinating part of the natural environment. They have majestic beauty and are located in wild and inaccessible mountain settings. Glaciers form when it is cold enough to allow snow to accumulate and _____ (slowly) change into ice.

2. Alpine climbing is a style of mountaineering that includes much of the equipment, technique, and safety precautions that are the basis for ice climbing and rock climbing. Alpine climbers are exposed to perils beyond their control, such as hidden _____ (very deep cracks; a break or wide and deep opening) and avalanches.

3. On their last afternoon on the island, Will looked at his Uncle John's shirt pocket and saw that it _____ (swelled outward) with treats. "Can I have one, Uncle John?" he begged. Uncle John pulled out a chocolate bar. "How about this?" Will took it gratefully. There had been no sweets on the island since that _____ (simple-minded person), the late governor, had banned most desserts.

4. On Saturday morning, May 3, 2003, two employees at the Franconia Notch State Park in New Hampshire noticed that the Old Man of the Mountain was gone. They could not see the _____ (projecting outward) rocks that have always defined his profile. His forehead and nose were missing. High winds and heavy rains had _____ (beaten; struck repeatedly) the rocks for several days. This, along with freezing temperatures, is thought to have contributed to the collapse.

5. Gloria had a _____ (tense; tightly stretched) smile. She had just been ordered by the Colonel to _____ (make a preliminary survey to gather information by exploration) the woods with her platoon. We entered the forest cautiously, but we began to move along at a fair clip, when Gloria, who was in the lead, gasped. She had stumbled over a wounded soldier lying _____ (face down on the supporting surface) in the damp soil.

Short Stories ~ (Textbook p. 134)

Name _____

A Boy and a Man

VOCABULARY

Activity 11

How Many Words Can You Find?

If you rearrange letters in each vocabulary word listed below, you will find other, shorter words within your vocabulary word. Make three words from each of your vocabulary words. Your words should have at least three letters.

For example, in the word *jutting*, you could find *jut*, *tut*, *tin*, *gin*, and *tint*.

We tell you how many words we found, but you will not know some of those words. If you are uncertain whether one of your made-up words is a real word, just look it up in the dictionary.

1. **bulge**
   We found 7 words: four 3-letter, two 4-letter, and one 5-letter.
   _____
   _____
   _____

2. **crevasse**
   We found 27 words: two 3-letter, ten 4-letter, eleven 5-letter, and four 6-letter. Because there is an *s* in *crevasse*, we were able to make plurals of many of our words. Because there is a second *s*, we were even able to make plurals of the words that already had an *s*.
   _____
   _____
   _____

3. **glacier**
   We found 28 words: ten 3-letter, twelve 4-letter, six 5-letter, and one 6-letter.
   _____
   _____
   _____

4. **gradually**
   We found 16 words: six 3-letter, eight 4-letter, and two 5-letter.
   _____
   _____
   _____

5. **imbecile**
   We found 8 words: one 3-letter, six 4-letter, one 5-letter, and one 6-letter.
   _____
   _____
   _____

6. **prone**
   We found 11 words: seven 3-letter and four 4-letter.
   _____
   _____
   _____

7. **pummeled**
   We found 14 words: four 3-letter, nine 4-letter, and one 5-letter past-tense word.
   _____
   _____
   _____

8. **reconnoiter**
   We found 25 words: eleven 3-letter, nine 4-letter, three 5-letter, and two 6-letter.
   _____
   _____
   _____

Short Stories ~ (Textbook p. 134)

A Boy and a Man

MORE ABOUT THE STORY
Writing Activity

Rudi's mother's desire to keep him safe is perfectly understandable. Even if her own husband had not died trying to scale the Citadel, she might very well not want her son involved in such a dangerous activity. The story does raise the theme, however, of whether it is better to follow our dreams—no matter how risky that may be—or whether one should stay safe. (And remember, safe does not necessarily mean settling for a job one dislikes.)

What do you think? How would you feel if your mother or father were involved in very high-risk activities? What if you, yourself, wanted to take on a job that involved risking your life, and your family objected? How should families and individuals resolve such differences?

Name _____

A Boy and a Man

MORE ABOUT THE STORY

Writing Activity

Short Stories ~ (Textbook p. 134)

A Boy and a Man

GRAPHIC ORGANIZER
Focus on Dialogue

The story opens with a minimum of narration. Almost all the information we need is presented to us in a series of questions and answers. This dialogue speeds up the pace of the story and begins building the tension and suspense right from the start. In the steps "down the mountain" there is a series of questions that Rudi asks Captain Winter. Complete the exercise by writing the answer to each question on the lines provided.

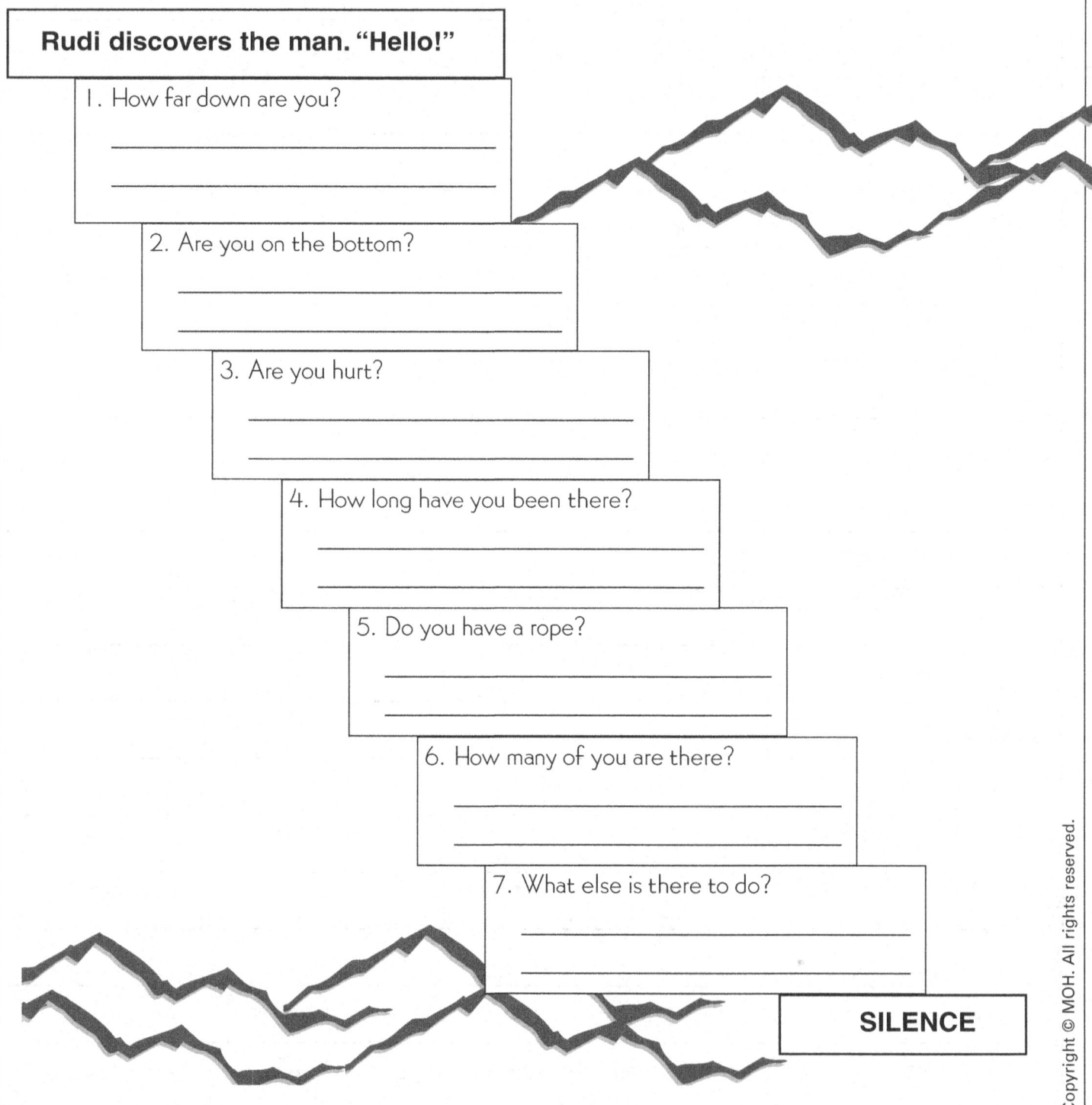

Rudi discovers the man. "Hello!"

1. How far down are you?
   _____
   _____

2. Are you on the bottom?
   _____
   _____

3. Are you hurt?
   _____
   _____

4. How long have you been there?
   _____
   _____

5. Do you have a rope?
   _____
   _____

6. How many of you are there?
   _____
   _____

7. What else is there to do?
   _____
   _____

SILENCE

Short Stories ~ (Textbook p. 134)

Name _____

A Boy and a Man

GRAPHIC ORGANIZER

Focus on Dialogue

As is often the case, a few moments of heroism seem like an eternity. Although the entire rescue takes only a short time, each step of it is critical to Captain Winter's survival. As each step is taken, the suspense is increased, as we don't know what the outcome will be. In the steps "up the mountain" you will find either a question or the description of an action. On the line under it, write Captain Winter's answer to Rudi's question or Rudi's response to Captain Winter's question or action. Again, notice how skillfully the author has built suspense through dialogue.

AND THEN IT WAS OVER.

7. Rudi began to lose his toe-holds.
   _____
   _____

6. Suddenly there was a jerk. The knot
   _____
   _____

5. Can you reach it?
   _____
   _____

4. How near are you now?
   _____
   _____

3. How far above you is it?
   _____
   _____

2. He removed his jacket...Can you see it now?
   _____
   _____

1. Can you see it?
   _____
   _____

He lowered the staff as far as it would go.

Short Stories ~ (Textbook p. 134)   85

The Hummingbird That Lived Through Winter

VOCABULARY
Activity 1

distinguish   pathetic   shaft   suspending

1. Sally looked in the direction of the river. There, on the nearest bank, she saw a _____ (pitiful) sight. She ran through the open field, down the muddy slope that led to the river. Would she get there in time?

2. People who are color-blind are usually born with the condition. Did you know that color blindness is much more common in men than in women? In fact, approximately one in 12 men has some problem with color perception. My brother has red-green color blindness, which means that it is very difficult for him to _____ (tell the difference between; separate from others, using some special feature) red from green.

3. Edward could not find his new tie. He especially wanted to wear it for his interview at the school. He looked everywhere in the house. Finally, he walked outside to his car. There it was. How could he have forgotten that he had _____ (hung) it from the mirror? Why is it, he thought, that you always find something in the last place you look?

4. The miners had been stuck below ground for nearly five days. One of the men commented, after they had finally been pulled to safety that, "It was the _____ (beam or beacon) of light that came through the hole on the surface—as well as the oxygen that came through with it—that enabled us to stay alive and keep our hopes up."

Name _____

The Hummingbird That Lived Through Winter

VOCABULARY

Activity 11

True or False?

Circle the correct answer.

1. When you cannot tell the difference between red and green,
   you cannot **distinguish** them from each other.   T or F

2. They were all having lots of fun.
   In other words, it was **pathetic**.   T or F

3. He pulled the sheet off the clothesline onto the ground.
   He was **suspending** it.   T or F

4. At the top of the domed ceiling, 100 feet above the marble floor where they stood,
   there was a circular opening that let in a **shaft** of light.   T or F

The Hummingbird That Lived Through Winter

MORE ABOUT THE STORY
Writing Activity

Seventeen species of hummingbirds breed in North America. Each species is different. The best clue to identification is the region where that hummingbird lives. Small "hummers," such as the Ruby-throated hummingbird, flap their wings about 55 times per second. Normal hummingbird flight speed is about 25 MPH.

All over the Americas, people build special feeders to attract hummingbirds. Tens of thousands of ordinary people track the migrations of the 300 species that can be found on the North and South American continents. Why are so many people so interested in these tiniest of birds?

Do some research, pick one hummingbird species to focus on, give the facts about it, and see if you can answer the question posed in the last paragraph.

_____
_____
_____
_____
_____
_____
_____
_____
_____
_____
_____
_____
_____

Short Stories ~ (Textbook p. 146)

Name _____

The Hummingbird That Lived Through Winter

GRAPHIC ORGANIZER

Identifying Elements of Plot

The Hummingbird That Lived Through Winter is a short, tightly woven story that follows a clear plan of exposition, climax, and resolution. In the **exposition**, the basic facts needed to set the scene for the story are presented to the reader. The characters are introduced, the setting is established, and other relevant details are given. In **rising action**, events based on the exposition and leading to the climax take place. The **climax** is the turning point of the story. In the **resolution**, the story's plot comes to a close. Problems are solved, mysteries are cleared up, and the fates of the characters are revealed.

In the exercise below, ten sentences have been quoted from the story. Next to each sentence, write Exposition, Rising Action, Climax, or Resolution to explain what role each of these sentences plays in the story's structure.

1. "It's dying," I said.
   _____

2. "Each of them is our bird," the old man said.
   _____

3. I expected the helpless bird to shoot upward out of his hand, suspend itself in space, and scare the life out of me—which is exactly what happened.
   _____

4. Across the street lived old Dikran, who was almost blind.
   _____

5. "I can't see, and the wife's not home."
   _____

6. I opened the window...and then it was gone.
   _____

7. After a moment the hummingbird began to show signs of fresh life.
   _____

8. "It is a hummingbird," I said half in English and half in Armenian.
   _____

9. The old man lifted his hand to his mouth and blew warm breath on the little thing in his hand.
   _____

10. This wonderful little creature of summertime in the big rough hand of the old peasant.
    _____

Short Stories ~ (Textbook p. 146)   89

The Sparrow

VOCABULARY — Activity 1

| alley | awe | frenzied | pace | stealthily |

1. John's manner was _____ (*desperately agitated*), as he tried to repair the damage he had done to the machine. He did not want to lose his job. He knew, too, that if he just relaxed, he had the expertise to fix it easily.

2. The older man and woman walked several miles each morning, often matching each other's _____ (*the rate of movement in stepping and walking*). They usually took the winding _____ (*path*) that provided a shortcut from their tenement to the park. It was their fifty-second year of marriage, and they loved being by themselves, away from the noise and dirt of the slum dwelling where they were forced to live.

3. Elizabeth was _____ (*had an overwhelming feeling of admiration for*) by the group of people. One by one, each went up to a homeless person asleep on the pavement. Some of the homeless men were very irritable, but she guessed she would be, too, if she had spent the night sleeping on the cement in the cold. She wanted to do this volunteer work, and followed their model of handing to each person a hot cup of coffee and a doughnut.

4. "What are we moving so _____ (*proceeding in a secret fashion*) for?" Alice asked. "I know we want to surprise them. But after all, we're not robbing a bank. And we don't want to scare them to death!"

Short Stories ~ (Textbook p. 152)

Fill in the Missing Words

1. When in silence I do sneak,
   because I want a private peek,
   I tiptoe softly down the stair—
   _____—watch out, beware!

2. She's agitated. Can't you see?
   Desperate. Rushing frantically.
   _____, frazzled, my oh me.
   Where oh where…is the key?

3. How fast can he walk?
   How fast does he run?
   David's _____ is
   the rate that he races,
   when he's having fun.

4. I followed the path in the park,
   a narrow _____, in the dark.
   Then I heard a big dog bark,
   and the singing of a lark,
   and the biting of a shark.
   Jack lit a match, some light, a spark.
   We shouted out, "Who goes there? Hark!"

5. Have you ever felt _____
   in the face of the law?
   Or given a cheer,
   when help was near?
   We're lucky, you know,
   because, wherever we go,
   the men in blue
   and women, too,
   can be found. It's true.
   Even in Kalamazoo.

The Sparrow

MORE ABOUT THE STORY

Writing Activity

> The Indian elephant, which is an endangered species, sheds tears when injured and when a family member is killed. It is well known that monkeys, chimpanzees, parrots, and dolphins that are kept alone for long periods develop illness. There are also hundreds of verified stories about animals demonstrating bravery. For example, a Labrador retriever barked for an hour in the snow to get help for a stranger who had fallen into a river. A cat in Hawaii led a woman to puppies that had fallen into a 12-foot-deep crack in the earth.
>
> Find such a story and retell it. Ask your teacher if you need help finding a source for this information.

_____
_____
_____
_____
_____
_____
_____
_____
_____
_____
_____
_____
_____
_____
_____

Short Stories ~ (Textbook p. 152)

Name _____

The Sparrow

MORE ABOUT THE STORY

Writing Activity

Short Stories ~ (Textbook p. 152)

The Sparrow

GRAPHIC ORGANIZER
Thinking Visually

Some things are so universally understood that they do not even require words to express them. As a matter of fact, some feelings can be more powerfully conveyed without words. Imagine that you had seen what the author of *The Sparrow* saw. Without a word being uttered, you would understand everything that the author understood.

In the six squares provided, draw six pictures, each representing one stage of the story. You will find that you need no captions at all to tell this universal story of a mother's love.

Name _____

The Sparrow

GRAPHIC ORGANIZER

Thinking Visually

1. There is an irony in the first line of the story; perhaps even the author was unaware of it. Can you explain what the irony is?
   _____
   _____

2. If the dog could talk, what do you think he would say about what happened and his part in it?
   _____
   _____
   _____

3. If the mother bird could tell her friends the story, how do you think she would describe the dog? The man? What she did? Her baby bird?
   _____
   _____
   _____
   _____
   _____
   _____
   _____

Short Stories ~ (Textbook p. 152)

Zoo

VOCABULARY
Activity 1

> breed   clutching   interplanetary   wonderment
> clustered   filed   jagged

1. My father regretted that _____ (*occurring between planets*) travel would not take place during his lifetime. He was always so curious about what we would find out there.

2. She focused the telescope, and motioned for me to look through the lens. "Do you see those stars, _____ (*gathered into a group or bunch*) near Orion's Belt?" I nodded. "That's where I come from, Betsy." I took a deep breath. Could she be telling me the truth?

3. We stood on several of the large _____ (*raggedly notched*) rocks that dotted the ridge. The night was silent and the moon silver. I heard the cry of an animal in the distance. I shivered with cold. Jim said, "Let's get back to the cabin and build a fire in the hearth." I was glad to leave that lonely place. As we headed down the hill, I tripped and fell to my knees. I looked up. My breath caught. I could not believe what I saw. I stared at the scene before my eyes with _____ (*amazement*).

4. They must have been an entirely different _____ (*kind; strain*) of creature. I was _____ (*holding tightly*) a large stick in my hands. Not that it would have made any difference. Not that I would have hurt any of them. But I was really scared. They looked like buffalo walking on their hind feet. We held still as they _____ (*marched in a line*) across the plain.

Short Stories ~ (Textbook p. 156)

Name _____

Zoo
VOCABULARY
Activity II

Now It's Your Turn

Use each one of the vocabulary words below in a sentence. You may use more than one sentence, if you wish, to provide a context for the word, so that it is clear you understand its meaning.

1. breed

2. clustered

3. clutching

4. filed

5. interplanetary

6. jagged

7. wonderment

Short Stories ~ (Textbook p. 156)

Zoo

MORE ABOUT THE STORY
Writing Activity

You are a Kaanian, one of the horse-spider beings of Kaan. You were among those who made the trip with Professor Hugo, to see the creatures in the zoo on Earth. Describe the Earthlings that you saw behind the bars. How are they different from you? How did you react to them? Are you glad you went?

Short Stories ~ (Textbook p. 156)

Name _____

Zoo

MORE ABOUT THE STORY

Writing Activity

Short Stories ~ (Textbook p. 156)

Zoo

GRAPHIC ORGANIZER
Point of View

A story's message often depends on who is telling the story. This lesson is driven home at the end of *Zoo*, when the point of view is suddenly changed. Learning to see things from more than one point of view is an important step in growing up. Teach yourself to stop for a moment and think—"this is the way I see it, but how does the *other* person see it?" You may be surprised at the answer.

In the exercise below, there are four "headlines." Write two stories for each headline. Write one from the point of view of one party named in the headlines, and write the second from the point of view of the other party named. Try to make the stories as different as possible, to illustrate how very important point of view is in reporting.

Mayor bows to the demands of sanitation workers for extra day off each month.

The Mayor	The Sanitation Workers

Short Stories ~ (Textbook p. 156)

Name _____

Zoo

GRAPHIC ORGANIZER

Point of View

Skiers, truckers, react differently to heavy snowfall in Midwest.

The Skiers	The Truckers

Summer vacation shortened by two weeks. Teachers feel math scores will improve. Students mournful.

The Teachers	The Students

Short Stories ~ (Textbook p. 156)

The Clearing

VOCABULARY

Activity 1

> *pruning   briers   hitch   heaps*

1. Jeff was irritated. According to his uncle's instructions, he should not have had any difficulty trying to _____ *(fasten)* the horses to the wagon. But this was his first time, and it was clear that the horses thought he was one very clumsy human.

2. I love to watch my grandfather working in his garden. Now that autumn is here, he has begun _____ *(trimming; cutting back)* all of the bushes. He has tried to teach me about gardening, but I fear I have not learned much. I still have not learned to handle plants without injuring myself on the _____ *(thorns; thistles)*. Of course, I don't complain about this. I don't want him to think I'm a baby.

3. My grandchildren are very pleased when I rake all the leaves together, so that they lie in _____ *(piles)* on the lawn. Then they run all the way across the yard, jump into the piles, and throw leaves and twigs at each other.

Short Stories ~ (Textbook p. 162)

Name _____

The Clearing

VOCABULARY

Activity II

Time to Rhyme

Next to each vocabulary word below, write five words that rhyme with it. Remember, the words do not have to be spelled the same way in order to rhyme. For example, *heaps* rhymes with *peeps*. Use the base word *prune*, instead of *pruning*, and *brier*, instead of *briers*, to make it easier.

The easiest way to check for rhymes is to go through the alphabet and try each letter to replace the initial consonant or consonants. Don't forget about double consonants, such as **cr**, **dr**, **sp**, **sh**, **sl**, and so forth.

1. **prune**   (for example, *moon*)
   _____   _____
   _____   _____
   _____

2. **brier**   (for example, *buyer, choir, inspire*)
   _____   _____
   _____   _____
   _____

3. **hitch**   (here, remember to try double consonants to replace the **h**, such as **sn**, **sw**, **tw**, **gl**, **st**, and **wh**)
   _____   _____
   _____   _____
   _____

4. **heaps**
   _____   _____
   _____   _____
   _____

Short Stories ~ (Textbook p. 162)

The Clearing

MORE ABOUT THE STORY

Writing Activity

> What could the family have done earlier in the story, to have changed the behavior of the Hinton boys? Pa asks, "But how are we ever going to know people like them?" Come up with an idea and write it down.

Name _____

The Clearing

MORE ABOUT THE STORY
Writing Activity

Short Stories ~ (Textbook p. 162)

The Clearing

GRAPHIC ORGANIZER
Analyzing Character

At the end of *The Clearing*, Pa and Mort Hinton become friends. Each has helped the other at a time of crisis. But it is not the crisis alone that helps them to become friends—it is the fact that each is a good man, and each is the type of man that the other one respects. Throughout the story, we see evidence of the good character traits of both families. Sooner or later, such good people are bound to become friends.

In the chart below, there is a list of twelve quotes. In a sentence or two, describe the character trait(s) reflected in the quote from the story.

Quote	Character Traits
1. "Wait until we get to know each other," Mom said.	1. *Mom is patient, kindhearted, and optimistic. She sees the good in people.*
2. I wanted to tell him that they would help his land. They'd get rid of insects that might destroy his crop.	2.
3. While Finn...cleared land on one side...the Hintons cleared on the other side.	3.
4. ...we found ourselves trying to do more work than four of them.	4.
5. "Don't answer him," Pa said.	5.

Short Stories ~ (Textbook p. 162)

Name _____

The Clearing
GRAPHIC ORGANIZER
Analyzing Character

Quote

Character Traits

6. "Your hens were on his land," Mom said. "He told you to keep off his land."

6. _____

7. "They're workers, all right," Pa said.

7. _____

8. "I'll be back when everything is all right," Mom said as she hurried off.

8. _____

9. "We've come to help," Mort said.

9. _____

10. We forgot about the rock fight. Now wasn't the time to remember it, when flames down under the hill were shooting twenty to thirty feet high.

10. _____

11. "How much do I owe you?" Pa asked Mort Hinton.

11. _____

12. Pa and Mort laughed and talked about weather and crops.

12. _____

Short Stories ~ (Textbook p. 162)   107

Home on the Range

VOCABULARY

Activity 1

armadillo   cordial   hillocks   mellow   sequestered

1. There was so much concern about the influence of media coverage during the trial that the jury was _____ (*secluded*). My daughter was an attorney on the defense team. I know she felt that it was important that the jury not be exposed to all the sensational coverage in the news. Of course, she does know that that sort of situation is very hard on the families of the jurors.

2. When the Stuarts moved to the neighborhood, they were delighted to find that everyone was so _____ (*friendly and warm*). The woman who lives next door gave them a loaf of home-baked bread. Another neighbor brought a bouquet of flowers. For the Stuarts, this was a new experience. They had just moved from a big city.

3. Did you know that _____ (*small insect-eating mammals with armor-like shells*) are mammals, not rodents or marsupials? They are not related to opossums, in spite of their similar appearance. Their shells are made of bone. How strange! There are twenty different kinds of armadillos, and I plan to get one for a pet. My mother thinks they look like artichokes.

4. When I was counting sheep last night to try to fall asleep, I could see little lambs frolicking in the _____ (*small hills*) of my mind.

5. I don't understand what people are talking about when they say that they are feeling _____ (*soft and gentle*). I am soft and gentle with babies and children, but that refers to how I treat them, more than to my general mood. Maybe when I get older, I'll know what that means. For now, I've got too much homework to do, and baseball practice every day after school.

Short Stories ~ (Textbook p. 170)

Name _____

Home on the Range

VOCABULARY

Activity II

What's Wrong with the Sentence(s)?

Explain what is wrong with the sentence(s) in the lines provided below the statement.

Example: When the cat purred and licked my arm, it was clear to me why Jane had said she was **unsociable**.
<u>A cat that is unsociable does not purr or make friendly overtures.</u>
<u>Unsociable means not being interested in friendly social relationships.</u>

1. I like having an **armadillo** for a pet, because she is so soft, cuddly, and furry.

2. After the Hinton boys threw rocks at me and my brother, Finn, I ran home and told my parents how **cordial** they had been.

3. Mt. Everest is a good example of a **hillock**.

4. The day that our house caught fire, we all felt really **mellow**.

5. I like to spend time with people, and don't like it much when I'm alone. So you can imagine how happy I was, when I learned that we were going to spend our vacation in a **sequestered** valley.

Short Stories ~ (Textbook p. 170)   109

Home on the Range

MORE ABOUT THE STORY

Writing Activity

Do you know what your mother or father does for a job? Your assignment is to interview either of your parents, and find out what he or she does at work. If your parent is a student, find out what he or she is studying. Think of good questions to ask, and write your questions down ahead of time. See if you can do your interview with your parent privately, so that you can both focus on it without distractions. Remember to get the specifics. Ask who they work for, what their job is called, and what exactly they do. You can also ask how they feel about their job. If your parent studies, you can ask the name of the school, what year of study this is for them, and what their day is like away from home.

Hopefully, both of you will have fun with this. Don't forget to write down the answers!

Name _____

Home on the Range

MORE ABOUT THE STORY

Writing Activity

Short Stories ~ (Textbook p. 170)

Home on the Range

GRAPHIC ORGANIZER

Writing Humor

Anything That Can Go Wrong, Will Go Wrong—Murphy's Law

Almost any routine job, in the hands of an expert at Murphy's Law, can take a turn for the worse! Let's have some fun and write a story similar to *Home on the Range*. Below, we have written the first part of the story. Write the rest of the story, incorporating Murphy's Law. Keep it funny—not tragic!

That morning I decided to bake bread. I'd never done it before, but we were expecting company that night and I was sure Mom would be pleased. I had the day off from school, but Mom was at work. The phone rang. It was Mom.

"Maureen," she said.

"Yes, Mom."

"I've got a few little things for you to do before Aunt Bea and Uncle Bill arrive. First of all, remember they're bringing the triplets."

"I remember, Mom."

"They can be a bit...unruly."

"I haven't forgotten, Mom."

"So be sure you hide all the vases, pictures, and knicknacks before those three-year-olds arrive."

"Okay, Mom."

"Also, they're bringing Walter."

Walter was their Clifford-size dog. Walter was huge, friendly, and lumbering.

"Maury," said Mom, using her nickname for me.

"Yes, Mom."

"Will you make a few side dishes for supper? I'm not sure I'll have time when I come home."

"Sure, Mom, what should I make?"

"It doesn't matter what you make, just remember not to use cinnamon, vanilla, or citrus."

"Why not?"

"Well, cinnamon makes Uncle Bill sneeze endlessly, vanilla makes Aunt Bea itch terribly, and any citrus fruit turns the triplets' skin a ghastly shade of yellow. It goes away, but it's scary."

Privately, I thought any change would improve the triplets, but all I said was, "Okay, Mom."

"Also, Maureen, be careful if you use the vacuum. It's been making funny noises and I'm not sure why."

"Okay Mom, I'll be careful."

"Thanks, sweetheart. I really appreciate your help. I sure do hope Uncle Bill and Aunt Bea don't arrive early..."

"Me, too, Mom. Bye bye. See you later. And don't worry. I'll have everything ready before you get home."

Short Stories ~ (Textbook p. 170)

Name _____

Home on the Range

GRAPHIC ORGANIZER

Writing Humor

Short Stories ~ (Textbook p. 170)

The Sound of Summer Running

VOCABULARY
Activity 1

> refraction   sinews   resilient   gazelles
> loam   limber   revelation

1. Have you ever stuck a stick halfway into a stream of water or a river or a pool? Did you notice that the stick looked as though it was bent at the point where it entered the water? This is what's called an *optical effect*—it's not really bending, it's your eyes that make you think it's bent. This visual impression is the result of _____ (*the deflection from a straight path that occurs when a ray of light passes from one medium, such as air, into another medium, such as glass*). As light passes from one transparent medium to another, it changes speed, and bends.

2. I think one of the keys to my grandfather's success in his garden was that he always used lots of _____ (*a soil consisting of an easily crumbled mixture of clay, silt, and sand*). The soil in my garden is too hard or too muddy. No plant could possibly want to grow there.

3. Jane saw that if she wanted to stay young and _____ (*flexible*), it would be a good idea to start taking yoga. Yoga would be gradual and relieve stress. It would stretch her _____ (*tendons*) without injury. After that, she could start walking each day, and she wouldn't have to worry about hurting her joints. Then, she could go on to running and aerobics! For a sixty-year-old, this was a very ambitious plan. But she had faith that she would do it.

4. Jane had read an article in a magazine that said that no matter what your age, you could greatly improve the condition of your body and your mind, if you started slowly and exercised regularly. For her, this was certainly a _____ (*an amazing, unexpected disclosure that created surprise*). Now, she could become more _____ (*flexible; elastic*). Why, she would be as graceful as a _____ (*small to medium swift African or Asian antelope*)!

Short Stories ~ (Textbook p. 184)

Name _____

The Sound of Summer Running
VOCABULARY
Activity II

Crossword Puzzle

Once again, we have indicated the definitions for your vocabulary words. Also, we have helped you out by putting some words in for you already. The definitions for these words are in bold. The puzzle is on the next page, and the down clues are on the following page.

ACROSS

4. an exclamation of irritation or anger
7. liquid inside a pen
8. **an amazing disclosure** *(vocabulary word)*
11. opposite of *out*
12. what you use to unlock a door
13. **strong or fortified places; permanent army posts**
14. the opposite of a *little*
15. **having wisdom and deep understanding**
16. the past tense of *run*
17. **stays still, expecting something to happen; stays still until something planned happens**
18. the scale that we sing: *do re me fa so la _____ do*
19. **a barrier that prevents the flow of water**
20. fuel that we use in our cars
22. short for mother
23. something that you ring
25. a preposition that tells where you are or were
26. fill in the missing pronoun: *he, she, _____*
27. **small, graceful antelope** *(vocabulary word)*
30. when you ingest food, you are _____
32. a body part that you hear with
33. **someone who is a relative is _____**
34. the opposite of daughter
35. a preposition meaning **to**ward:
    "Over the river and through the woods, _____ grandmother's house we go"
36. the opposite of old; the opposite of used
37. if you work for someone, that person is your _____

Short Stories ~ (Textbook p. 184)   115

The Sound of Summer Running

VOCABULARY — Activity II

Crossword Puzzle

Short Stories ~ (Textbook p. 184)

Name _____

The Sound of Summer Running

VOCABULARY

Activity II

DOWN

1. tendons *(vocabulary word)*
2. opposite of uncles
3. bending of a ray of light *(vocabulary word)*
4. red building where animals are kept on a farm
5. abbreviation for **att**orney
6. opposite of hers
8. flexible, elastic *(vocabulary word)*
9. one of the two body parts used for seeing
10. a soil mixture *(vocabulary word)*
11. **an infinitesimal amount**
12. "Let's go fly a _____!"
14. flexible *(vocabulary word)*
20. **look at intently**
21. past tense of eat
23. something you read
24. what a hen lays
26. contraction of 'it is'
28. contraction of 'let us'
29. **a country in Southeast Asia, northeast of Thailand, west of Vietnam**
31. abbreviation for **n**orth**n**orth**e**ast

Short Stories ~ (Textbook p. 184)   117

The Sound of Summer Running

MORE ABOUT THE STORY
Writing Activity

> Think of something in your life, or something that you want, that gives you—or you think would give you—great pleasure. What is it? It can be a kind of food, a piece of clothing, shoes, a toy or game, a book, a camp you want to go to, having privacy and being alone to do something by yourself. In other words, it can be something you want to have or something you want to do. For a title, write what this "thing" or this experience is. Then, go on to describe it. Try to talk about it both realistically *and* fancifully, just as Ray Bradbury has written what a pair of sneakers mean to a particular boy at a particular time of year.

Name _____

The Sound of Summer Running

MORE ABOUT THE STORY

Writing Activity

Short Stories ~ (Textbook p. 184)

The Sound of Summer Running

GRAPHIC ORGANIZER
Interpreting Metaphors

In *The Sound of Summer Running*, fantasy weaves in and out of reality. Sneakers have a life of their own and take on magical powers. The author employs metaphors and metaphorical writing to create the fantasy part of the story.

What is a metaphor? A metaphor is language which compares one thing to another without using the word "like" or "as." For example, if one wishes to say "the grass feels like velvet" one could write, metaphorically, "the grass is velvet." Ray Bradbury takes the use of metaphor to an extreme by moving in and out of metaphors without warning.

In the chart below, eleven of the story's metaphors are quoted. The page on which each metaphor is found is included so that you can go back to the story and see how the metaphor was used. In the column next to the metaphor, identify the item being compared and the object, feeling, or idea to which it is being compared. In the last column, interpret the metaphor. Explain what the author is trying to say through the metaphor. For example, if the author has written "the grass is velvet," you would interpret: the grass is soft to the touch the way velvet is.

The Metaphor	Object Compared/ Compare to	Interpretation
1. ...the special shoes that were quiet as a summer rain falling on the walks. (p. 185)	1. *shoes/summer rain*	1. *Sneakers silently hit the pavement just as light rain silently falls to the ground.*
2. the grass was still pouring in from the country (p. 185)	2.	2.
3. Any moment the town would capsize (p. 185)	3.	3.
4. They put marshmallows and coiled springs in the soles (p. 186)	4.	4.

Short Stories ~ (Textbook p. 184)

Name _____

The Sound of Summer Running

GRAPHIC ORGANIZER

Interpreting Metaphors

The Metaphor	Object Compared/ Compare to	Interpretation
5. Somewhere deep in the soft loam of the shoes (p. 186)	5. _____	5. _____
6. ...peel off the iron leather shoes (p. 186)	6. _____	6. _____
7. Shoes like these could jump you over trees and rivers and houses. (p. 186)	7. _____	7. _____
8. Feel those shoes...All those springs inside? Feel all the running inside? (p. 188)	8. _____	8. _____
9. The tennis shoes silently hushed themselves deep in the carpet (p. 188)	9. _____	9. _____
10. The boy looked down at his feet deep in the rivers (p. 189)	10. _____	10. _____
11. "Antelopes," said Mr. Sanderson. "Gazelles." (p. 189)	11. _____	11. _____

Short Stories ~ (Textbook p. 184)

The Circuit

VOCABULARY

Activity 1

galvanized   savoring   surplus

1. My son was trying to use his vocabulary words in everyday conversation. He figured that *that* way, he would really learn the words. Yesterday afternoon, I asked what he would like for dinner. Jim said, "Well, Mom, what I would really _____ (relish; enjoy) would be some ground beef."

2. "Hamburgers?" I laughed because of the words he was using. "I think I may be able to arrange that. Know why? Because, young man, in this household we have a _____ (superabundance) in the meat department. Especially since your sister became a vegetarian last week."

3. Sam talked to his son-in-law, who is the vice president of Mid-America Steel. What in the world was meant by _____ (plated with zinc to resist rust) steel? David gave him a two hour lecture about how the zinc keeps the steel from getting corroded and about how the steel is produced. Actually, it was very interesting, but I was embarrassed when I saw that Sam had fallen asleep.

Name _____

The Circuit

VOCABULARY

Activity II

More Word Analogies

In the word analogies below, two ask for antonyms (or words of opposite meaning) and one asks for a synonym.

1. *good* is to *bad*, as **surplus** is to
       a. too little   b. a lot   c. a superabundance

2. *liking* is to *disliking*, as **savoring** is to
       a. relishing   b. enjoying   c. not enjoying

3. *sofa* is to *couch*, as **galvanize** is to
       a. cup   b. plate   c. dish

Short Stories ~ (Textbook p. 192)

The Circuit

MORE ABOUT THE STORY
Writing Activity

The dictionary entry for the word *circuit* is very long. For this assignment, you may either (1) carefully write down all of the definitions; or (2) pick one of the more specific definitions (for example, *circuit judge, circuit breaker, circuit rider, closed-circuit,* or *circuit board*) and see what information you can find out about it. Write one or two paragraphs about what you found out.

Name _____

The Circuit
MORE ABOUT THE STORY
Writing Activity

The Circuit

GRAPHIC ORGANIZER

Evocative Language

The Circuit is about hopelessness and hope. Panchito, the hero of the story, has been born to a life of poverty from which his parents cannot escape. For him, though, there is one escape route—that route is education. But, there's a catch. His poverty keeps him from getting an education, which is why the story is called *The Circuit*. Panchito goes from hopelessness, to hope, and back to hopelessness.

As you read the story, certain phrases and visual images highlight the hopelessness or hope that the hero feels. From the group of phrases and objects at the bottom of the next page, select the ones that reflect the hopelessness of Panchito's situation and place them in the chart on the left. Then select the phrases and objects that reflect hope and place them in the chart on the right.

Hopelessness			

Short Stories ~ (Textbook p. 192)

Name _____

The Circuit

GRAPHIC ORGANIZER

Evocative Language

Hope			
			And then: …when I opened the door to our shack, I saw that everything we owned was neatly packed in cardboard boxes.

1. ya esora
2. Webster's dictionary
3. the dirt floor, populated by earthworms
4. clock set at 8:00
5. tienen que tener cuidado
6. school buildings
7. the walls eaten by termites
8. school desk
9. an old jalopy
10. jug of water
11. "May I help you?"
12. a beat-up old pot
13. having to move to Fresno
14. school bus
15. pile of books
16. a trumpet

Short Stories ~ (Textbook p. 192)

Home

VOCABULARY

Activity 1

| obstinate | shafts | saffron |
| emphatic | flat | hurl |

1. David would not change his mind about doing a jigsaw puzzle. His sister, Melissa, was terribly disappointed. "I don't understand you," she cried. "I always try to do what you want. It hurts my feelings. Why are you so incredibly _____ (stubborn)?"

2. "What can I say?" David responded. "What I really feel like doing is washing and drying the dishes, because Mom asked me." Melissa looked at him, not quite believing what she was hearing. "You know what? You are strange," she said _____ally (definitely). "Well, I think I will just take the puzzle and _____ (throw) it out the window."

3. They lived with their parents in a nice _____ (apartment). It was an old building. In fact, once it had been a factory warehouse, so the windows were enormous. Also, _____ (beams) of light came in through the skylights. Melissa sat down, discouraged, on the long _____ (orange-yellow)-colored sofa, with her head in her hands. She had already finished her homework. David looked at her and felt bad. "Okay, okay," he said. "I'll do the puzzle with you. Just give me a few minutes to do the dishes first."

Short Stories ~ (Textbook p. 202)

Name _____

Home
VOCABULARY
Activity II

Pick the Synonym

Four words are listed below each vocabulary word. Select the word that means the same thing (or nearly the same thing) as the vocabulary word.

1. **obstinate**
    cooperative
    angry
    mean
    stubborn

2. **emphatic**
    difficult
    definite
    deceitful
    delicious

3. **hurl**
    curl
    storm
    throw
    hit

4. **flat**
    house
    apartment
    sidewalk
    table

5. **shafts**
    winds
    chimneys
    chutes
    beams

6. **saffron**
    color
    yellow-orange
    apron
    blue-green

Short Stories ~ (Textbook p. 202)

Home

MORE ABOUT THE STORY
Writing Activity

Have you ever heard the saying or the idiom, *Home is where the heart is*? What do you think this means? Write about it.

_____
_____
_____
_____
_____
_____
_____
_____
_____
_____
_____
_____
_____
_____

Name _____

Home
MORE ABOUT THE STORY
Writing Activity

Short Stories ~ (Textbook p. 202)   131

Home

GRAPHIC ORGANIZER
Details Create Atmosphere

In *Home*, the author describes the home that the characters in the story fear they will lose. A sense of the house and how much it means to the three women is created by listing many small details about the house. In each of the circles provided, write one detail mentioned about the house and draw a picture of it as you think it looks.

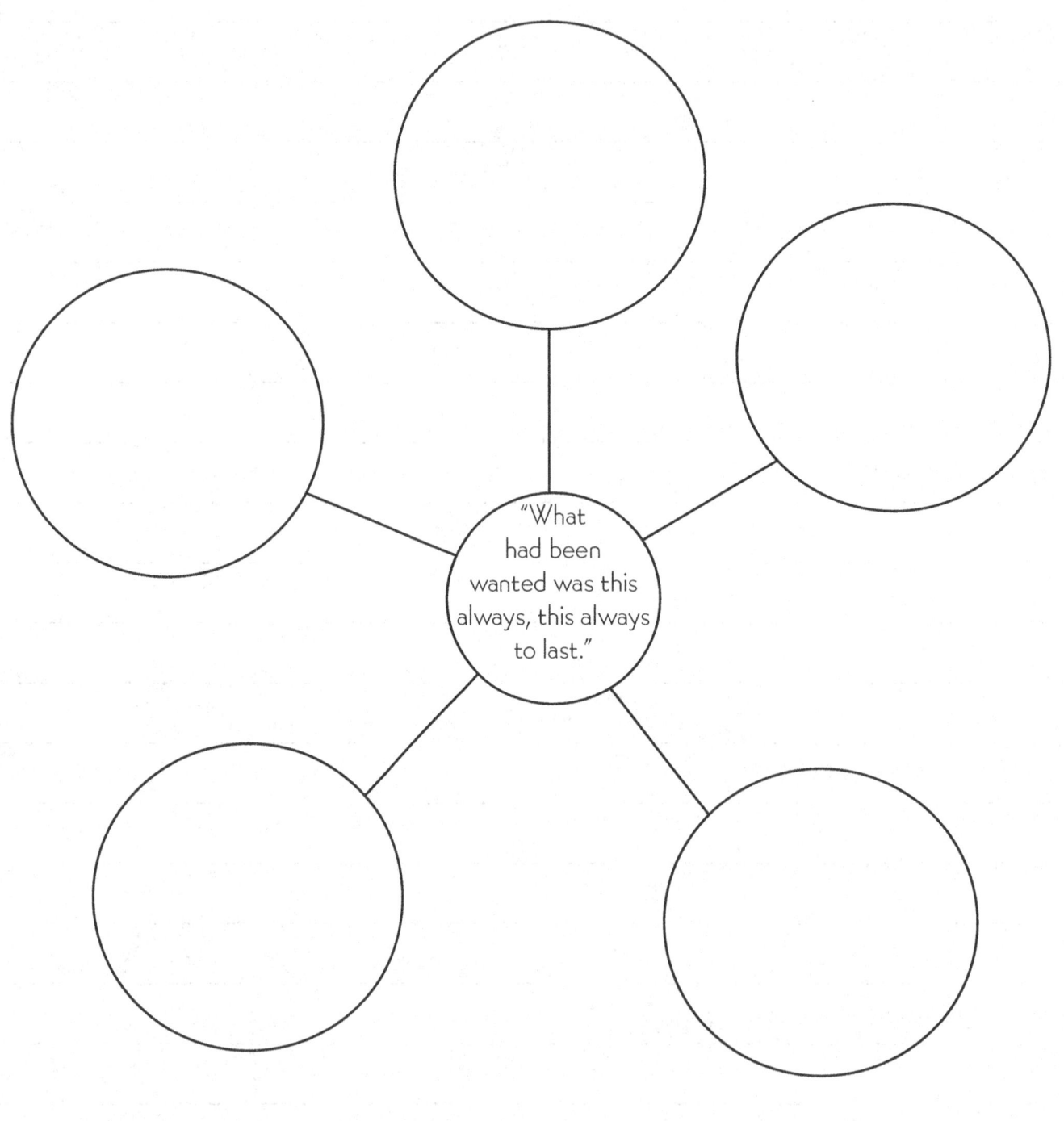

Short Stories ~ (Textbook p. 202)

Name _____

Home

GRAPHIC ORGANIZER

Details Create Atmosphere

Imagine sitting on the porch or lawn of your house. Looking around, what do you see? What parts of your home would you be most reluctant to leave? In each of the circles below, draw a picture of a precious part of your home or yard, and write a caption underneath it.

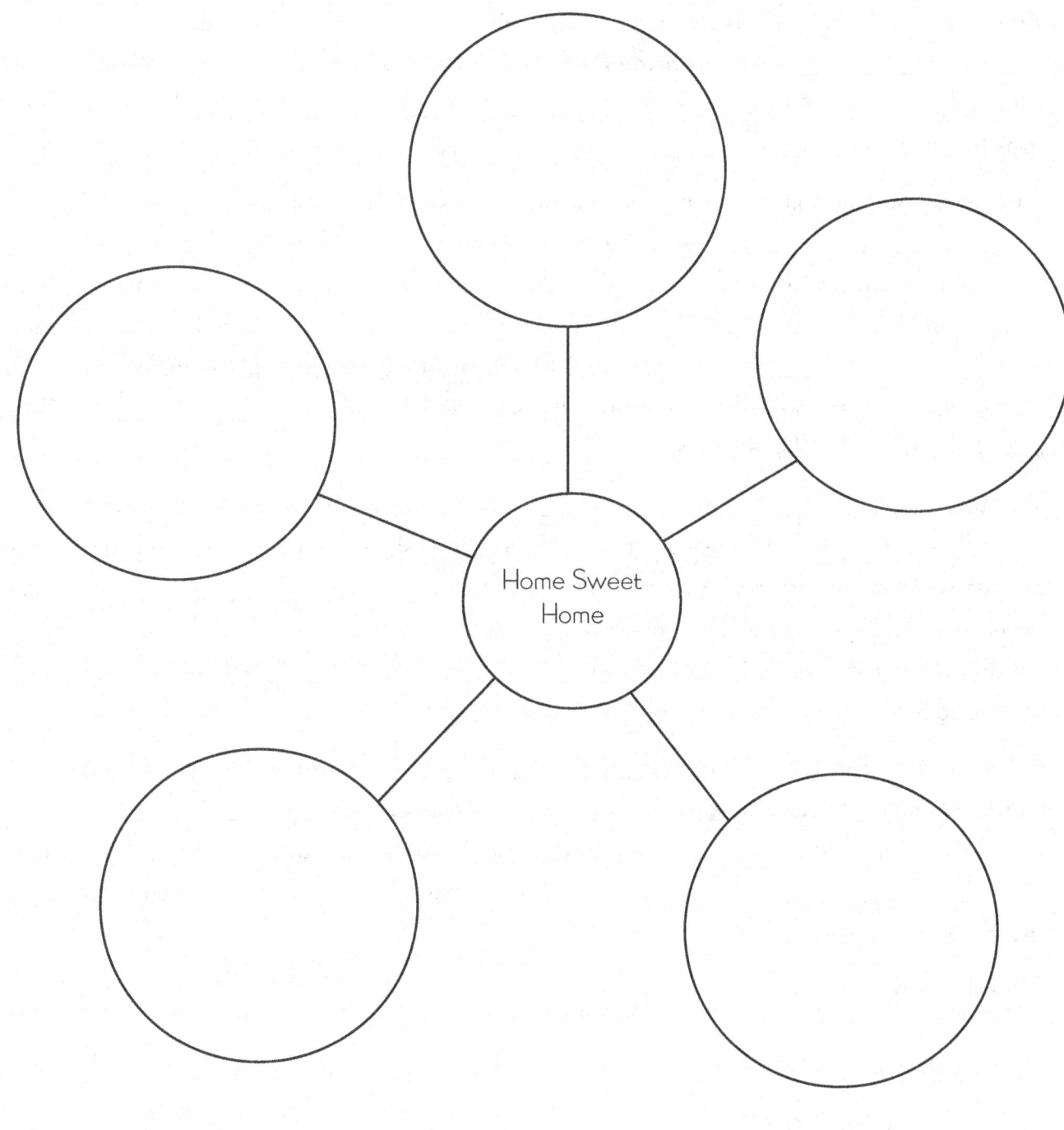

Short Stories ~ (Textbook p. 202)   133

Child Pioneer

VOCABULARY
Activity 1

aloof	clouted	gleaned	profusion	writhes
barren	derelict	pathos	seasoned	
brutal	epic	pestilence	staggering	

1. You could tell that Edward would not have been the sort of person you would want to spend time with. It is clear to me from reading his published diaries, and the information I have _____ (gathered) from biographies, that Edward had a short temper. He was constantly screaming at his students and _____ (hitting) them. Don't you think that he was _____ (cruel; harsh; cold-blooded)?

2. George always claimed that Martha, his sister, was very kind but definitely _____ (reserved). But who could blame her? They had grown up as orphans, raised by an uncle who lived in the Australian Outback. They had no neighbors and no other children with whom they could play. The Outback, as you may know, is a strange place. The desert is near and _____ (desolate), as you might expect. It is a place where you can feel very lonely. The one time Henry and I visited, I was filled with _____ (feelings of pity) for the children.

3. The story was a(n) _____ (heroic) tale of a woman pioneer who had crossed the country and experienced great hardship. When she arrived at the home of her sister and brother-in-law, she found only a few starving animals and a(n) _____ (abandoned) shack. She drove the old wagon twenty miles back to town, where she learned that every member of the family had died during the _____ (plague). She had come too late to help!

4. A person who is in great pain may _____ (twist) in agony. When a person hasn't had enough to eat or is feverish, they may walk unsteadily, or _____ (reel from side to side; walk with a faltering step; sway). Obviously, it takes a(n) _____ (experienced) doctor or physician's assistant to recognize and treat the symptoms of illness.

5. After the heavy rain, the _____ (abundance) of flowers was glorious!

Short Stories ~ (Textbook p. 208)

Child Pioneer

VOCABULARY

Activity II

Name _____

Learning the Words

    Child Pioneer has thirteen listed vocabulary words. Will you remember what they mean? Will you remember how to spell them? Some of these words are very difficult to get a sense of. From the list below, pick six words. For each of your words,

    1. give the part of speech (noun, verb, adjective) *as the word is used in your textbook;*

    2. give the definition from your dictionary—for that part of speech; and

    3. use the word in a sentence. Have your dictionary open when you begin the exercise.

aloof	brutal	derelict	gleaned	pestilence	seasoned	writhes
barren	clouted	epic	pathos	profusion	staggering	

1. Word _____ Part of speech _____
   Definition _____
   Sentence _____
   _____

2. Word _____ Part of speech _____
   Definition _____
   Sentence _____
   _____

3. Word _____ Part of speech _____
   Definition _____
   Sentence _____
   _____

4. Word _____ Part of speech _____
   Definition _____
   Sentence _____
   _____

5. Word _____ Part of speech _____
   Definition _____
   Sentence _____
   _____

6. Word _____ Part of speech _____
   Definition _____
   Sentence _____
   _____

Short Stories ~ (Textbook p. 208)

Child Pioneer

MORE ABOUT THE STORY
Writing Activity

> Pick one of the events or episodes in *Child Pioneer*, and write a journal entry of several paragraphs for John, Francis, or the eight-year-old sister. Remember to use the first-person voice ("I"). Give your entry a date, and if you can, a location.

Name _____

Child Pioneer

MORE ABOUT THE STORY

Writing Activity

Short Stories ~ (Textbook p. 208)

Child Pioneer

GRAPHIC ORGANIZER
Focus on Character

Young John Sager is one of those rare human beings who are so determined, so clear-minded about their goal, that nothing short of death can stop them. Throughout the story, one valid reason after another to abandon the journey presents itself to John. Yet, he never wavers in his determination to reach the Columbia Valley.

In the diagram on these two pages, we have likened John Sager's spirit to a straight arrow. We have likened all the reasons to turn back to gusts of wind, trying to blow the arrow off course. On the gusts of wind write the reason John might have turned back. In the arrow you will find what he actually did in the story.

1. Both parents had died.

2.

3.

1. The Sager orphans stay with the caravan until it reaches Fort Hall.	2. John decided to go on to the Columbia River.	3. John and the children cross the Snake River Valley.	4. John leaves Fort Boise, taking the baby with him.	5. The children cross the Blue Mountain with no guides.

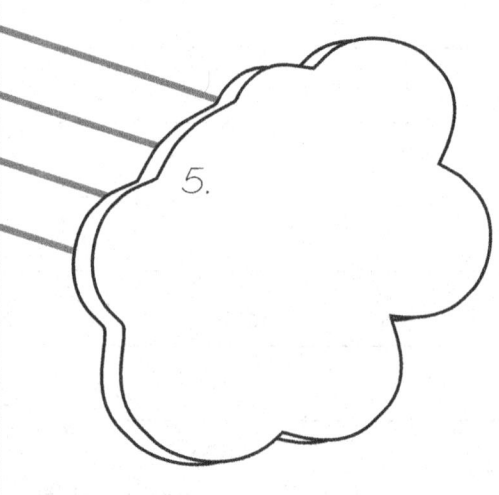

5.

6.

Short Stories ~ (Textbook p. 208)

Name _____

Child Pioneer

GRAPHIC ORGANIZER

Focus on Character

4.

| 6. The children begin the last lap of their journey. | 7. The baby is revived. | 8. John and all his siblings make a home for the Sager family. |

7.

Short Stories ~ (Textbook p. 208) 139

The Runner

VOCABULARY

Activity 1

| consternation | inexorable | lariat | phosphorescent | roan |
| forage | inherent | nonplused | prodigious | |

1. I have always been _____ (*puzzled; unsure of*) by human reasoning. Forests are cut down, so that humans can build more houses and new towns. Not surprisingly, the animals who have always lived in the forest experience _____ (*amazement or dismay that hinders or throws into confusion*). They lose their homes, their territory, and their sources of food. Nonetheless, the few species that survive—raccoons and skunks, for example—are a source of irritation and complaint to the humans. Fortunately, however, these survivors are able to _____ (*search for food*) in trash cans.

2. We humans think that the skunks smell. Imagine what they think of us! Granted, we are surely an _____ (*unyielding*) force. Therefore, we are able to do whatever we want as a species, even if it results in vast environmental devastation. Certainly, it will take a(n) _____ (*immense; extraordinary size*) effort to repair even a small part of our destruction of the natural world.

3. Have you ever seen _____ (*glowing*) life-forms in the ocean or on the beach at night? Chuck and Tom argued during class about whether these life-forms were plants or animals. George said that it was odd that such a glow is _____ (*inborn*) in a life form's physical makeup. Sidney agreed with him. But Phil thought it wasn't surprising. "What about fireflies?" he asked. I just think that anything that glows is really beautiful.

4. Jeannie's family has many horses. Even though she is only ten, she is able to snag her favorite horse, Galloper, a _____ (*brownish-red colored horse*), with her _____ (*rope*). Susan admires and envies her. She complains that she has practiced and practiced, and she still can't do it.

Short Stories ~ (Textbook p. 216)

Name _____

The Runner

VOCABULARY

Activity II

Play the Association Game!

In learning new words, it helps to make associations with words or expressions we already know. In the exercise below, two words or expressions can be associated with, or are synonyms for, the vocabulary word. One term is not. Circle the two synonyms or associated terms. Now, choose one of them and use it in a sentence (or two) with the vocabulary word. Use a dictionary for this exercise.

Example: **consternation** (a.) dismay (b.) confused fright c. relaxation
When Jill was lost in the maze, she experienced consternation. You can hardly blame her feeling dismay, when she could not find her way out.

1. **roan**   a. a horse   b. calico cat   c. brownish-red
   _____

2. **inherent**   a. outside   b. genetic (from the genes)   c. inborn
   _____

3. **phosphorescent** a. glowing   b. dark as night   c. luminous
   _____

4. **forage**   a. eat   b. to wander looking for food   c. search
   _____

5. **prodigious**   a. small   b. extraordinary in degree   c. immense
   _____

6. **inexorable**   a. yielding   b. never give up   c. unyielding
   _____

7. **nonplused**   a. plus   b. puzzled   c. perplexed
   _____

8. **lariat**   a. lasso   b. necklace   c. rope
   _____

Short Stories ~ (Textbook p. 216)   141

The Runner

MORE ABOUT THE STORY
Writing Activity

Some people seem to just naturally feel sympathy for their fellow creatures. Others of us may develop such feeling through experiences of our own as we grow up. How does a trapped animal feel? Pick an animal that is hunted by man. Give the animal a good name. Now write, either in the third-person voice (he, she, it) or the first-person voice (I), how it feels to be trapped.

Name _____

The Runner
MORE ABOUT THE STORY
Writing Activity

Short Stories ~ (Textbook p. 216)

The Runner

GRAPHIC ORGANIZER
Sense of Time

The Runner takes place over two days. To Shadow, these days must have seemed like weeks, for he worked and worried almost every minute of the forty-eight hours. The author wants us to be aware of the time of day, for it is frequently mentioned.

To complete the diagram below, describe what was happening in the story during each section of time indicated on the "clock." The two clocks take you through the first 24 hours of the story.

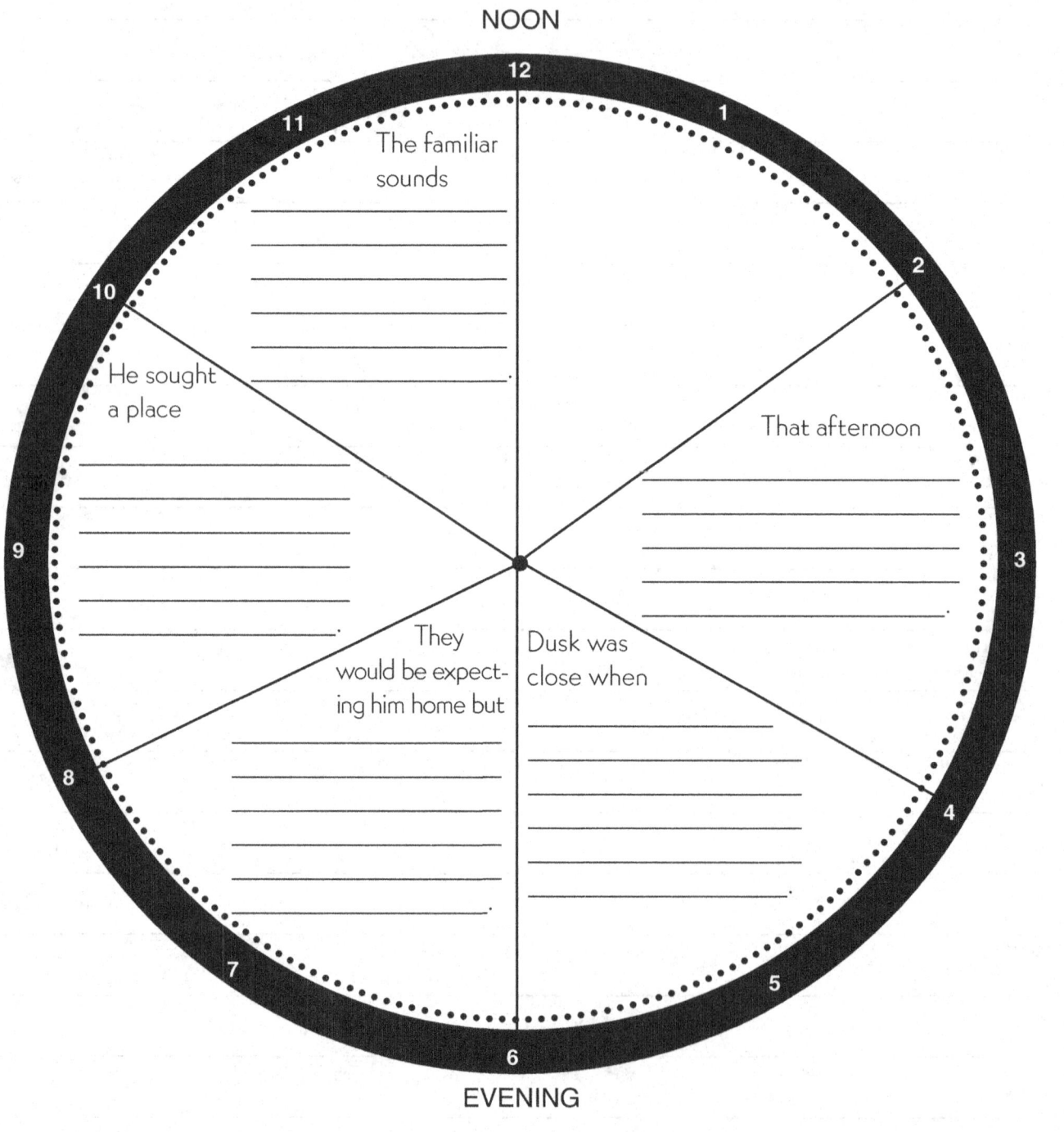

Name _____

The Runner

GRAPHIC ORGANIZER

Sense of Time

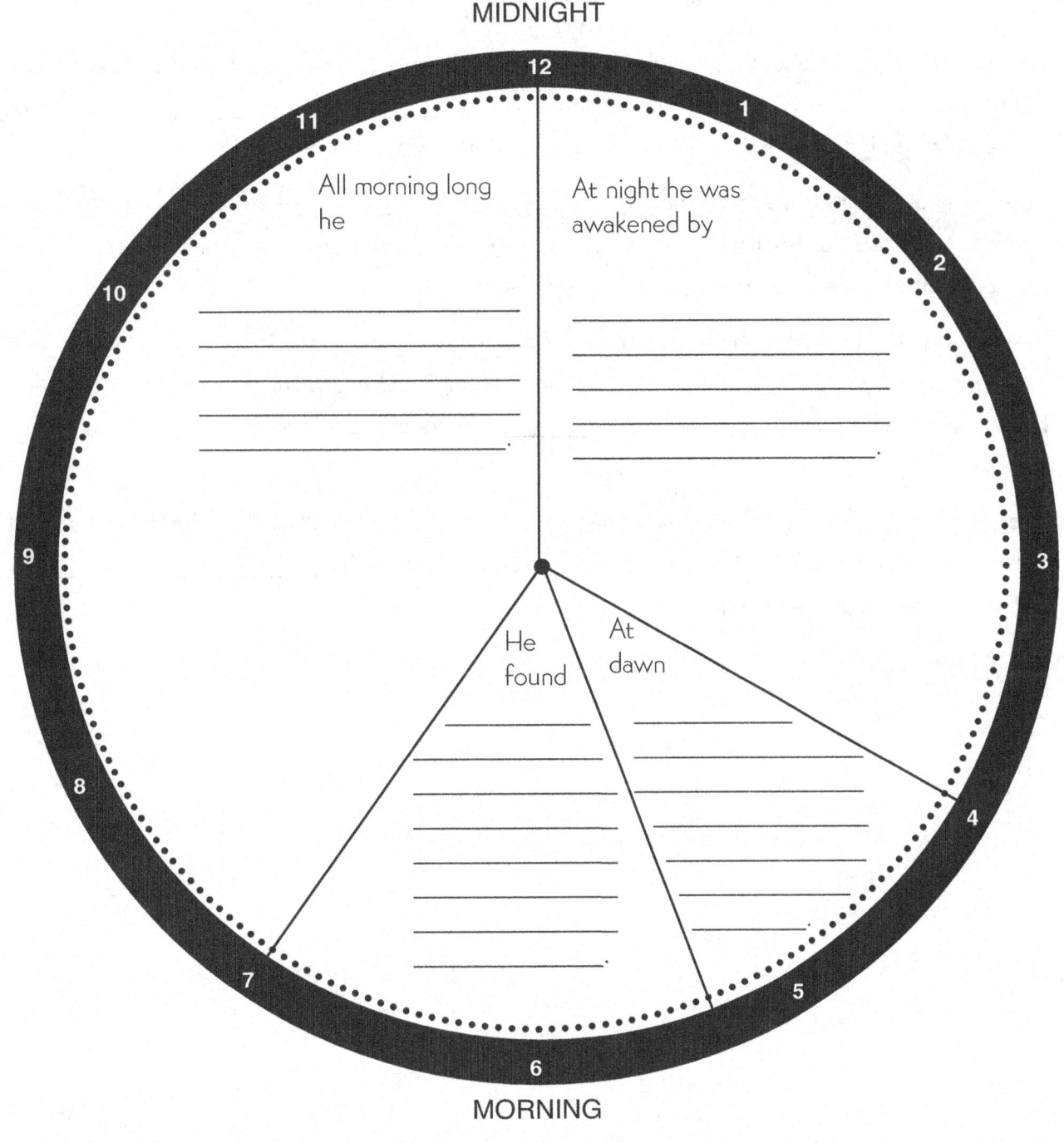

Short Stories ~ (Textbook p. 216)

After Twenty Years

VOCABULARY
Activity 1

egotism   spectators   stalwart   swagger   vicinity

1. Greg could only think about his own feelings. Because he was so warm and friendly, those who got to know him well were eventually surprised by his _____ (self-importance). He seemed so kind. But he was unable to consider the needs of other people.

2. The prosecutor called twenty of the _____ (onlookers; one who looks or watches) into court to testify as witnesses. But they told twenty different stories. I have since learned that eyewitness testimony is not very reliable.

3. In spite of all the hardships she had to endure, Amelia never gave up. As Greta reminded us, Amelia had been _____ (having outstanding strength) to the very end. Hundreds of friends who lived in the _____ (area; neighborhood) attended the memorial service.

4. Sean grew up in the slums of Manhattan and always was a bit of a bully. Maybe he did this so that no one would bother him. He acted like a tough guy and walked with a _____ (an air of overbearing self-confidence).

Short Stories ~ (Textbook p. 230)

Name _____

After Twenty Years

VOCABULARY

Activity II

Write a Story Using Your Vocabulary Words

If you are going to tell a tale of approximately four paragraphs, and you want to include your five vocabulary words, you may have to tell a TALL tale. Your plot can be silly, but you need to sensibly connect these words to each other.

Use a dictionary to get a broader sense of what the following words mean: *egotism, spectators, stalwart, swagger, vicinity.*

_____
_____
_____
_____
_____
_____
_____
_____
_____
_____
_____
_____
_____
_____
_____
_____
_____
_____
_____
_____
_____
_____
_____
_____

Short Stories ~ (Textbook p. 230)

After Twenty Years

MORE ABOUT THE STORY
Writing Activity

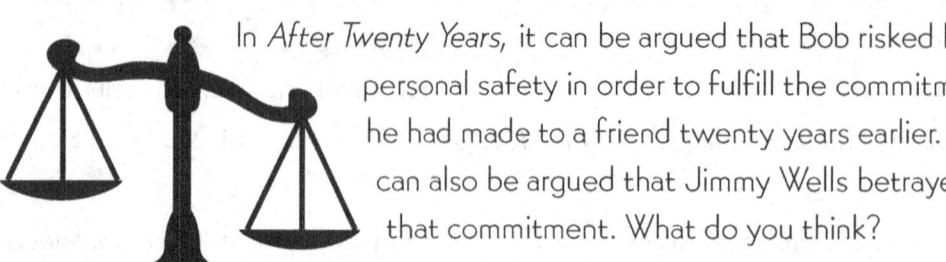

In *After Twenty Years*, it can be argued that Bob risked his personal safety in order to fulfill the commitment he had made to a friend twenty years earlier. It can also be argued that Jimmy Wells betrayed that commitment. What do you think?

Name _____

After Twenty Years

MORE ABOUT THE STORY

Writing Activity

Short Stories ~ (Textbook p. 230)

After Twenty Years

GRAPHIC ORGANIZER

Visual Symbols

This O. Henry story, like many of his stories, is about the struggle between good and evil. The good people in O. Henry's world are usually steadfast, modest, and quietly noble. In this tightly woven story, the contrast and interplay of good and evil are played out against a background of light and dark. Throughout the story, the author uses flashes of light against the darkness to mirror the flashes of good that dispel the evil in this world. As the story progresses, the reader is provided with scenes, in each of which the dark is dotted with points of light. In the final scene, no mention of the dark is made. The scene is acted out in a pool of light.

In the exercise below, you will find boxes representing the six "scenes" of *After Twenty Years*. In the darkened box, you will see phrases from the scene that describe the darkness. On the right hand side, write down phrases from that "scene" of the story that describe light or objects (such as a diamond or a lighted cigar) that illuminate the darkness.

The Avenue

1. The time was barely ten o'clock.
2. ...business places that had long since been closed...

1. *the lights of a cigar store*
2. _____

Where Big Joe Brady's used to stand

1. The doorway of a darkened hardware store
2. an unlighted cigar in his mouth

1. _____
2. _____
3. _____
4. _____

Name _____

After Twenty Years

GRAPHIC ORGANIZER

Visual Symbols

The agreement twenty years ago

1. We agreed that night that we would meet here again.

1. _____

After the policeman leaves

1. There is now a fine, cold drizzle falling.

1. _____

The two men meet

1. The two men started up the street, arm in arm...The other submerged in his overcoat, listened with interest.

1. _____

Under the light

The dark is now illuminated by JUSTICE.

When they came into this glare each of them turned simultaneously to gaze upon each other's face.

Short Stories ~ (Textbook p. 230)   151

Cat on the Go

VOCABULARY
Activity 1

apprehensive	emaciated	inevitable	ploy
articulating	excursions	inoculation	sentimental
benevolent	gash	meticulously	uncomprehendingly

1. The family was very poor. There was never enough to eat. The children's clothes were ragged, and they were _____ (very thin; wasting away physically; malnourished). When Sam arrived at school for the first day, the teacher stared at him _____ (unable to understand). Mrs. Green, who was very _____ (having or showing tender feelings) about her students, went to the principal's office and started to cry.

2. Mrs. Cabot, the principal and her boss, was a stern but _____ (kind) person. She could be tough with her teachers, but she could also be relied upon to be caring with the students. Mrs. Green was so upset, however, that she was having trouble describing what she had observed about Sam. "I'm sorry, Mrs. Cabot," she said, "but as you can see I'm having trouble _____ (pronouncing distinctly; giving clear and effective utterance to; putting into words) my feelings."

3. Mrs. Cabot, however, understood. "The father's been out of a job and is having trouble getting work. The mother is ill. There are eight children to feed. I have been _____ (worried; anxious) about this situation since I met the family last week." She handed Mrs. Green a tissue. "I do know that the children have had their _____ (vaccinations)."

4. Mrs. Green nodded. "But we have to find a way, a _____ (tactic), to get food to the family, without insulting them. Also, Sam has a _____ (cut; wound) on his forehead and I worry that it's infected." She sighed deeply.

5. Mrs. Cabot stood and walked over to her file cabinet. "Listen. We will give the situation very special attention. Don't worry. We will deal with all of this _____ (very carefully, with attention to details). I have already arranged for you to distribute a snack to your class twice a day. In the meantime, enjoy Sam. He's a lively boy and a good boy."

6. Sam *was* a good boy and a good student. He took advantage of every opportunity to learn more. When Mrs. Green told the class that they would be going on a trip to Wild Animal Farm, Sam could hardly contain his excitement. He raised his hand and said, "You mean all of us? You mean we're all going on a(n) _____ (brief pleasure trip)?" Mrs. Green smiled. She supposed it was _____ (unavoidable) that she would come to really enjoy this appreciative boy.

Nonfiction ~ (Textbook p. 352)

Name _____

Cat on the Go

VOCABULARY

Activity II

Etymology Again

Remember, *etymology* teaches us about the origins of words. For this exercise, you will need a dictionary that gives the origin of the word, in addition to the definition. Your job is to look up four vocabulary words, and write down the information that tells where the word came from. See page 51 for a list of abbreviations used in the dictionary to explain the origin of a word.

Let's take one of your vocabulary words, *uncomprehendingly*. For this word, we need to look at the base word, *comprehend*. Here, the prefix *un-* means *not*.

The dictionary says that the word is from Middle English, from Latin *comprehendere*, from *com-* + *prehendere* to grasp. The Latin prefix *com-* means *with* or *together*.

Now you try it. If you need, ask your teacher for help.

1. *meticulous* comes from _____
2. *benevolent* comes from _____
3. *gash* comes from _____
4. *inevitable* comes from _____

Most dictionaries give the word root information only for the base word. For example, *inhumane* has no information about the origin of the word, but its opposite, *humane*, which is the base word, has information about the source of the word. Sometimes it is hard to figure out from the original word why a word means what it does today.

Cat on the Go

MORE ABOUT THE STORY
Writing Activity

The cat is an animal perfectly designed for survival. Cats are mischievous, reserved, and dignified. Domestic cats are now the most popular species to have for a pet in the United States. What do you know about cats? If you own a cat, this is your opportunity to write about your pet. If not, do some research on cats, and write about something you find interesting.

Name _____

Cat on the Go

MORE ABOUT THE STORY

Writing Activity

Nonfiction ~ (Textbook p. 352)

Cat on the Go

GRAPHIC ORGANIZER
Charting Relationships

James Herriot's beloved stories are about a country veterinarian, the animals he treats, and the people of Yorkshire, England, among whom he lives. The remarkable kindness that Herriot observed as he made his daily rounds leaves the reader with a warm glow.

Cat on the Go can be divided into three parts. The first part includes the cat's discovery, surgery, and eventual healing. The second part is his life with the Herriots, the third, his life with the Gibbonses. In each section, Oscar/Tiger is treated with exceptional kindness by the humans in his life. Oscar cannot physically help the many people who help him, and yet he gives them all they want in return: his affection.

In the exercise below, you will find one drawing representing each of the three periods in Oscar's life. In some of the blank circles, you will fill in the names of the people who helped Oscar and briefly describe what each did for him. Some of the circles are about people who helped other people, and one is about Oscar helping a person. Fill in those circles as well and briefly describe the kindness done.

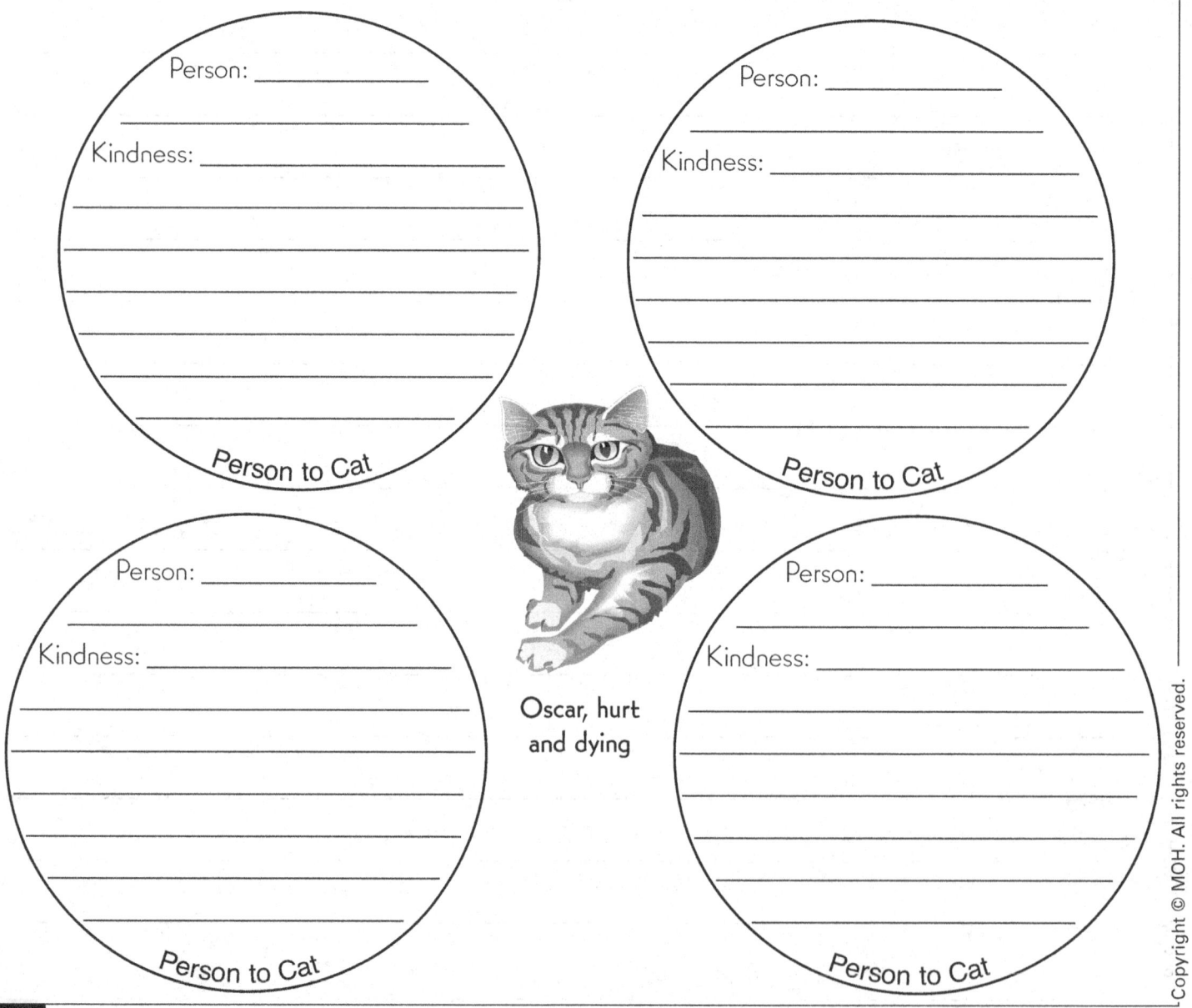

Oscar, hurt and dying

156   Nonfiction ~ (Textbook p. 352)

Name _____

Cat on the Go

GRAPHIC ORGANIZER
Charting Relationships

Person: _____
_____
Kindness: _____
_____
_____
Person to Cat

Person: _____
_____
Kindness: _____
_____
_____
Person to Cat

Person: _____
_____
Kindness: _____
_____
_____
People to People

At the Herriot household

Person: _____
_____
Kindness: _____
_____
_____
Person to Cat

Person: _____
_____
Kindness: _____
_____
_____
Person to People

At the Gibbons household

Person: _____
_____
Kindness: _____
_____
_____
Cat to People

Nonfiction ~ (Textbook p. 352)

The Night the Bed Fell

VOCABULARY
Activity 1

| irritable | notion | perilous | prowling |
| juncture | ominous | phobia | vague |

1. She was unable to leave the house, because of her _____ (intense fear) of open spaces and of strangers. Usually her family was very patient with her, but sometimes it made them _____ (upset and impatient). They would try to reason with her. "Please just try going out. You'll see that nothing out there is so _____ (dangerous)."

2. Her father tried to dismiss the _____ (idea) that there was something to fear. "Nothing out there is so _____ (threatening), Maria."

3. Maria cried, "I can't explain. I have these _____ (not clearly expressed; not clearly defined) feelings of danger. I know how silly it sounds. But it's as if there's someone or something _____ (roaming about in a sneaky way) around out there."

4. Maria got on a program at home of meditation and exercise. She cut out sugar and caffeine from her diet. She was really very brave about it, and she got a lot of support from her family and friends. When spring came, and the days started to grow longer, she began a garden. She would force herself to go out in the yard each day. It was at this _____ (point in time) that curiosity, loneliness, and the desire to be out with her friends helped her take the final step. And now she's just fine!

Name _____

The Night the Bed Fell

VOCABULARY

Activity II

Circle the word that is different from the other four. If there is a word you don't recognize, use the dictionary. You should also check each vocabulary word in the dictionary, to see if it has other definitions besides the ones given in your textbook.

1. **vague**
   cloudy
   indefinite
   focused
   unclear

2. **phobia**
   fear
   cold feet
   fearlessness
   dread

3. **perilous**
   safe
   dangerous
   unsafe
   risky

4. **juncture**
   point in time
   connection
   joint
   disjuncture

5. **notion**
   concept
   motion
   whim
   idea

6. **ominous**
   forbidding
   doomful
   joyful tidings
   threatening

1. Who might **prowl about**?
   _____
   _____

2. What could cause someone to be **irritable**?
   _____
   _____

3. What kind of situation could be **perilous**?
   _____
   _____

4. Do you have any "odd **notions**"?
   _____
   _____

5. At what **juncture** in your life do you think you will be an adult?
   _____
   _____

Nonfiction ~ (Textbook p. 366)   159

The Night the Bed Fell

MORE ABOUT THE STORY
Writing Activity

> We laugh when people exaggerate. For example, if you had an unpleasant morning, to be funny you might say, "It was the worst morning of my life! I felt like boulders were falling from the sky." It is also funny when people say the opposite of what is true. For example, if it takes you a long time to wake up, you might say, as James Thurber does in *The Night the Bed Fell*, "I told him that I was such a light sleeper that if anybody quit breathing in the same room with me, I would wake instantly." What is funny with both exaggeration and stating the opposite, is the obvious ridiculousness of the statement.
>
> Below, write four statements. Two will be exaggerations. Two will be the opposite of what's true. After each, write a sentence saying what is really true.

The Night the Bed Fell

GRAPHIC ORGANIZER

Focus on Humor

Mixed Nuts

The cast of characters in *The Night the Bed Fell* are an assortment of odd, but harmless, characters. As we begin to read, so many eccentric figures are thrown at us, that it's difficult to remember which "character" is which. We have designed a small chart for you, to help you keep track of the cast of characters. In the exercise below, in each box, there should be a name and a description of one character. We have filled in some of the information—you fill in the rest.

Name of Character	Description
1.	1. She feared the bed's headboard would crash down and kill someone.
2. Grandfather	2.
3.	3. He needed to sleep in the attic in order to think.
4. Briggs Beall	4.
5.	5. He claimed he was a very light sleeper but was really the opposite.
6. Old Aunt Melissa	6.
7. Aunt Sarah Shoaf	7.
8.	8. She scared off burglars each night by hurling shoes down the hall.

Nonfiction ~ (Textbook p. 366)

Barrio Boy

VOCABULARY
Activity 1

> anchorage   formidable   persistently
> contraption   maneuvered   radiant

1. They always spoke of Igor in whispers. He had a problem with his temper. He was easily insulted, too. But people were mostly scared of Igor because of his _____ *(threatening; causing fear or dread)* strength. Simone had once seen him crush a boulder.

2. One day, someone saw Igor smile. No one had ever seen Igor smile before. Who could have _____ *(to manage or move into or out of a position)* the young giant, and *how*, so that he actually felt happy!

3. And, if you can believe it, Igor's smile was _____ *(shining)*!

4. When they observed him more closely, William, Marvin, and Harry saw that Igor was smiling down at a gray mouse. With his large fingers, he kept touching an object hanging from his neck. What was this pendant? What sort of _____ *(device; gadget)* could it be?

5. We talked about it among ourselves for several days. Our parents complained that we were gossiping, being unfair to Igor, who really had a lonely life. But we were really curious. And we were also gossips. We talked about Igor _____ *(relentlessly; continuously in the face of opposition; stubbornly)*.

6. But it became clear that Igor had really changed. He was happy. He was friendly. He showed us his mouse. I was talking to my father about it one night. He said, "Maybe having a pet has given Igor _____ *(security; something that can be firmly relied on)*. Perhaps he needed a friend." My father is very wise.

Name _____

Barrio Boy

VOCABULARY

Activity II

Using Your Dictionary and Thesaurus

Words, as you know, can have several different meanings. Sometimes you will get a better sense of a word if you read all its definitions in the dictionary. Well, here's your chance. For this exercise, you will need a dictionary and a thesaurus. First, give at least two definitions for the word. *Maneuver* can be defined as a noun or a verb. Make sure you define it as a verb. Then, check in your thesaurus for two synonyms. If you don't understand the definitions in the dictionary, ask for help.

anchorage   Definition: _____
                             _____
                Synonyms: _____

contraption Definition: _____
                             _____
                Synonyms: _____

formidable   Definition: _____
                             _____
                Synonyms: _____

maneuver   Definition: _____
                             _____
                Synonyms: _____

persistent   Definition: _____
                             _____
                Synonyms: _____

radiant   Definition: _____
                             _____
                Synonyms: _____

Barrio Boy

MORE ABOUT THE STORY
Writing Activity

In *Barrio Boy*, the author says that his teacher, Miss Ryan, patiently helped him with "the awful idiocies of the English language" (p. 374). Some of the awful idiocies of the English language surely are spelling that has *nothing* to do with pronunciation. (Of course, English is not the only language like this!)

Can you find ten English words that are not pronounced the way they are spelled? Here are some clues. Look for words that begin *gn* and *kn*; words that end *-ght*; and words that end *-ough*. Can you think of a rank of army officer, in which an *l* is pronounced like an *r*?

Name _____

Barrio Boy
MORE ABOUT THE STORY
Writing Activity

Nonfiction ~ (Textbook p. 372)

Barrio Boy

GRAPHIC ORGANIZER

Clarifying Some Rules of English

Learning English is the immigrant's passport to success in America. This is no easy task. English is full of all kinds of exceptions and oddities which trip up the foreigner at every turn. A major obstacle to learning English is the fact that the same word can sometimes have several different meanings. In the chart below, you will find a few of the many questions a foreigner might ask you about the English language. Answer them to the best of your ability. If you do not know the answer, ask your teacher or some other adult for help.

What your friends ask you	What you answer
1. I see the word *set* used in three different ways. Can you write one phrase for each of the different ways in which it is used?	1.
2. I'm not sure when to say *lie* and when to say *lay*. Can you give me a simple rule?	2.
3. Is *flammable* the opposite of *inflammable*?	3.
4. What about *valuable* and *invaluable*? Which has more value, an object that is valuable or one that is invaluable?	4.
5. Do pitted prunes have pits or not?	5.
6. The plural of dear is _____. What is the plural of deer?	6.
7. What word rhymes with **tough**? With **cough**? With **through**? With **bough**? Who made up these rules anyway???	7.

Name _____

Barrio Boy

GRAPHIC ORGANIZER

Clarifying Some Rules of English

8. What rhymes with **bus**? What rhymes with **busy**? What rhymes with **bury**? What rhymes with **bull**? (I'm moving to France!)	8. _____
9. What is the opposite of *indelible*?	9. _____
10. Is an infamous person someone who is famous or not famous? If not, what is he?	10. _____
11. What is the difference between **aisle** and **isle**?	11. _____
12. Is there a difference between *envelop* and *envelope*?	12. _____
13. Can *farther* and *further* be used interchangeably?	13. _____
14. What about *toward* and *towards*?	14. _____
15. Can you explain the difference between *uninterested* and *disinterested* to me?	15. _____
16. List three more "idiocies of the English language" of your own choosing!	16. _____

Nonfiction ~ (Textbook p. 372)

Helen Keller

VOCABULARY
Activity 1

| augmented | devoid | reflecting | vibrations |
| detecting | ratified | tenacity | vitality |

1. Sylvannah woke up each morning _____ on *(thinking about)* her good fortune. Violette, her enormous Rottweiler, lay at the foot of her bed. Orangey, her orange cat, purred on her pillow. What more could anyone desire?

2. She had traveled with her mother, Betsy, out of a war zone. They had survived, because of their _____ *(perseverance)*.

3. She recalled one day, long ago, when her mother had awakened early. Betsy had _____ *(discovered)* telltale sounds. Sylvannah had felt the _____ *(shaking movements)* of soldiers on the march. They had left most of their belongings behind, but they had fled to safety.

4. Her world had been _____ *(expanded)* with their arrival in the U.S. She found she had greater _____ *(energy)* in her new surroundings. Sometimes, of course, she remembered the terrible things she had seen and felt life was _____ *(empty)* of meaning.

5. When she learned a peace treaty had been _____ *(approved; upheld)* in the country of her birth, she felt inner peace.

Nonfiction ~ (Textbook p. 378)

Name _____

Helen Keller

VOCABULARY

Activity II

Find the Opposite

Draw a line from the vocabulary word to the word or phrase that is its opposite.

vibrations	full
reflecting	unable to discover
detecting	giving up easily
vitality	acting impulsively, without thought
devoid	still; without movement
ratified	shrank
augmented	vetoed
tenacity	lacking energy

Find the Synonym

Now draw a line from the vocabulary word to its synonym.

tenacity	increased
vibration	finding out; observing
detecting	vim and vigor
devoid	thinking about
ratified	holding onto
reflecting	without; empty
augmented	shaking
vitality	approved

Nonfiction ~ (Textbook p. 378)

Helen Keller

MORE ABOUT THE STORY
Writing Activity

 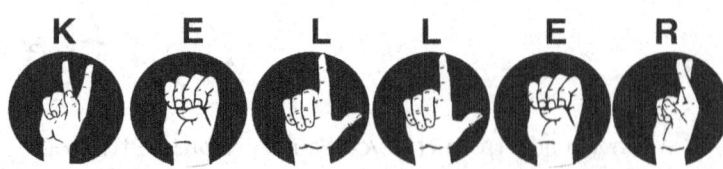

> In this brief biography, you learn an odd assortment of information about Helen Keller's accomplishments. Do some research, and write three paragraphs either about Helen Keller, Anne Sullivan, or the system of communication Anne Sullivan developed to "speak" with Helen Keller. Try to include information that is not given in the selection you have just read.

Nonfiction ~ (Textbook p. 378)

Name _____

Helen Keller
MORE ABOUT THE STORY
Writing Activity

Nonfiction ~ (Textbook p. 378)

Helen Keller

GRAPHIC ORGANIZER

Focusing on the Senses

Because two of her senses were cut off, her three remaining senses were augmented, not the sense of touch alone but the sense of taste and the sense of smell.

Helen Keller amazed and inspired the world with her spirit, her determination, and her brilliance. As we read the story, we learn of the many things she "saw" and "heard." We almost forget that she was blind and deaf, so "normal" are her reactions to sights and sounds. Yet, all her perceptions of what things looked like, or how they sounded, came through her senses of touch, smell, and taste. In the exercise below, you will see a list of many things Helen Keller "saw" or "heard" through her other senses. On the opposite page, you will find a pyramid divided into three. Place the phrases that tell how she saw or heard something through her sense of touch into the bottom section of the pyramid. Into the middle section, copy the phrases which tell how she saw or heard something through her sense of smell. At the top of the pyramid, write down the phrase which tells how she heard or saw something through her sense of taste. Two of the phrases can be listed in both "touch" and "smell."

Helen Keller:

- saw the Medici tombs
- heard a Yankee twang
- saw a woman's makeup
- saw white lilacs
- heard people walking upstairs
- read maps
- read the Bible
- selected ripe blueberries
- distinguished weeds from flowers
- listened to Beethoven's symphonies
- could tell it was night
- understood the idea of sweet and bitter
- saw a painter on a bus

Name _____

Helen Keller

GRAPHIC ORGANIZER
Focusing on the Senses

Sense of Taste

1. _____
   _____
   _____

1. _____
   _____
2. _____
   _____
3. _____

Sense of Smell

1. _____
2. _____
3. _____
4. _____
5. _____
6. _____
7. _____
8. _____
9. _____
10. _____

Sense of Touch

Nonfiction ~ (Textbook p. 378)

Roberto Clemente: A Bittersweet Memoir

VOCABULARY
Activity 1

> battered   delineate   prominent   tragically   virtually
> conjectured   gesturing   resented   undercurrent

1. The cats and dogs had gathered in the woods. Orangey stepped forward. "What is the purpose of this meeting, good ladies and gentlemen?" "_____ (sadly), Little White Foot, kitten and friend, has disappeared," Mr. Woof answered.

2. Mr. Purr spoke softly to Mrs. Bow-wow. "Do you think Little White Foot took some foolish risk?" he _____ (guessed).

3. Bow-wow kept it to herself, but she _____ (felt annoyed with) the suggestion. "Oh, come on," she said. "Surely, Little White Foot is _____ (almost entirely) one of our most safety-minded kittens—even if she is very playful!"

4. They looked up to see Sally Spaniel _____ (motioning) to everyone for quiet. Now, there was an _____ (a force that is not readily visible) of tension among the canines and felines grouped about under the trees.

5. Patrick the Poodle stood. "All of us have noticed recently that some of the trees and rocks have been _____ (worn or damaged by hard usage or by blows). Of course, we all assumed it was the ferocious wind."

6. One of their most _____ (widely or popularly known; standing out) citizens raised her hand. Patrick called on her. "I, for one, do not accept the Weather Theory. I believe that the battered trees and rocks, and the disappearance of Little White Foot, have the same cause. Please let me _____ (describe in detail) my own theory. Then we can make a plan for the rescue of Little White Foot." A sigh of relief broke through the audience.

Roberto Clemente: A Bittersweet Memoir

VOCABULARY

Activity 11

Name _____

What's Wrong with the Sentence(s)?

Each sentence misuses a vocabulary word. Explain what's wrong with the sentence, by writing what the vocabulary word is *supposed* to mean. Please use a dictionary, in addition to the textbook definitions.

Example: Jim knew the answer to the question, so he **conjectured**.
Wrong! Conjectured means guessed. Jim would not guess if he knew the answer.

1. **Tragically**, he has lived a long, wonderful life and has many great accomplishments.
   Wrong! _____

2. The walls of my room look beautiful, since they have just been repapered and replastered. That's why my friends say that the walls are so nicely **battered**.
   Wrong! _____

3. Jane **resented** it, when Betty told her she was so glad to meet her.
   Wrong! _____

4. Sean hadn't been there at the time of the accident. So we were all glad to listen to him **delineate** the events that occurred.
   Wrong! _____

5. IRV72**, the robot, was a computer that could not move. Therefore, we liked to watch it **gesturing** as it told a story.
   Wrong! _____

6. No one had ever heard of Bartholomew. He was one of the most **prominent** beavers living in the dam.
   Wrong! _____

7. Bob yelled, "Here comes an **undercurrent** of bad feeling! I can see it!"
   Wrong! _____

8. The twins did not look anything alike. They were **virtually** identical.
   Wrong! _____

Nonfiction ~ (Textbook p. 386)   175

Roberto Clemente: A Bittersweet Memoir

MORE ABOUT THE STORY
Writing Activity

Roberto Clemente was very successful in his field. He was a talented ballplayer. He had opportunities that many people never have. He seems to have been a person of good character. Is the story of Roberto Clemente really a tragic one? Begin your essay with the sentence, "Roberto Clemente's story is a tragic one." Or, if you don't think so, start with "Roberto Clemente's story is not a tragic one." Then, give the reasons for your conclusion in two or three paragraphs.

Name _____

**Roberto Clemente:
A Bittersweet Memoir**
MORE ABOUT THE STORY
Writing Activity

Roberto Clemente: A Bittersweet Memoir

GRAPHIC ORGANIZER
Focus on Writing

Jerry Izenberg, the author of the essay about Roberto Clemente, was a sportswriter. He refers briefly to several events in the life of Roberto Clemente. In all likelihood, many newspaper columns were written about each of these events.

In this exercise, you will find six "headlines" based on events referred to in the story. On the lines below the headlines, write a column or press release about the headline. Draw upon information in the story, your own knowledge, or your imagination to give details to the story. Do your best to write like a sportswriter.

Pedro Zarilla's New Rookie: Roberto Clemente. Can He Play?

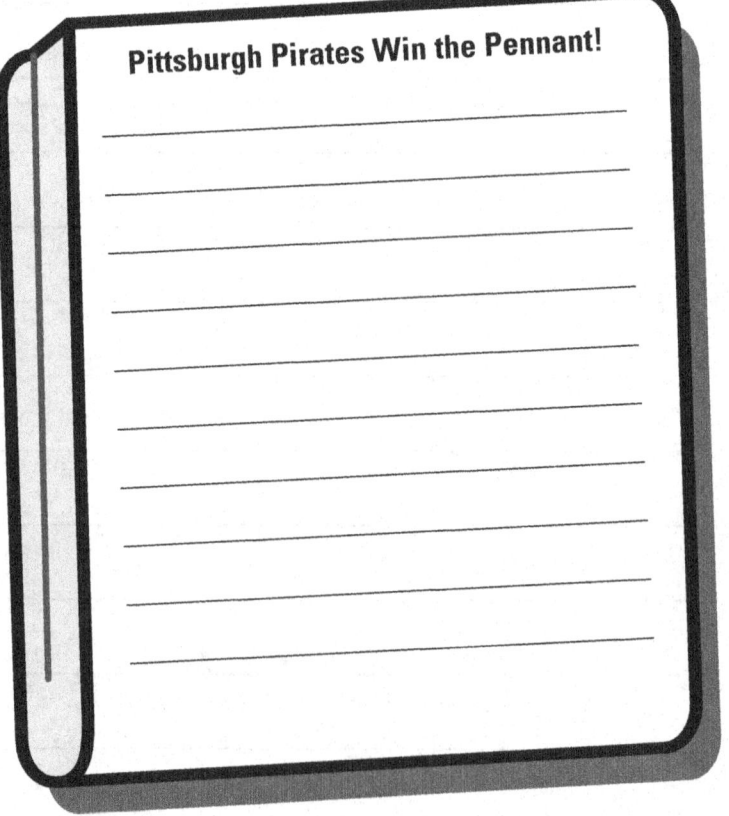

Pittsburgh Pirates Win the Pennant!

Nonfiction ~ (Textbook p. 386)

Name _____

Roberto Clemente: A Bittersweet Memoir

GRAPHIC ORGANIZER

Focus on Writing

An Interview With Maria Isabella Casares, Clemente's Teacher

Earthquake Demolishes Managua— Clemente to the Rescue

Goods Not Getting to Nicaragua

Mission of Mercy Plane Disappears; Clemente on Board

Nonfiction ~ (Textbook p. 386)

Florence Nightingale

VOCABULARY
Activity 1

> bigots   converse   innovation   prerogative   uniform
> chaos   efficiency   miscellaneous   sturdy
> consented   fatigue   ordeal   skeptics

1. James walked home late that night, very _____ (tired; exhausted). He didn't like his job. He had _____ (agreed) to work there, because he needed the money.

2. But he found he could hardly _____ (talk with) with the other employees. He had heard them gossip and make cruel remarks about other workers. Well, he supposed they were just a bunch of loudmouths and _____ (people with prejudices).

3. The factory, itself, was poorly organized. He found it hard to accomplish anything in such _____ (a state of utter confusion). The management would get an **F** for _____ (effectiveness), if anyone were grading them.

4. They did not use any of the technological _____ (new ideas, methods, or inventions) available. There were _____ (various; diverse) machines and systems they could have brought on line.

5. The new technology could have meant _____ (firmly built; strong) products. Quality would have been _____ (having the same form; alike), no matter the skill of the individual worker.

6. So what? Who was he to complain about the management? If the owners thought they were saving money this way, it was certainly their _____ (privilege; option).

7. The company CEOs were _____ (doubters), when anyone talked of modernization.

8. James knew he couldn't go on working in a place that he hated. Every day was a(n) _____ (trial). He would have to find a way to go back to school in the evenings, although it would be hard on his wife and children. When he thought of them waiting for him at home, he remembered what a lucky man he was. He felt less tired. He quickened his pace.

Nonfiction ~ (Textbook p. 396)

Name _____

Florence Nightingale

VOCABULARY

Activity II

Another Chance to Do Word Analogies

Remember to figure out the relationship between the first pair of words, in order to find a match in the second pair. Use a dictionary!

1. **bigots** is to **spigots** as **bill** is to _____
   a. beak   b. spill   c. skill   d. invoice
   Clue: This one has nothing to do with the meaning of the words!

2. **chaos** is to **order** as **war** is to _____
   a. peace   b. battle   c. winter   d. fighting

3. **consented** is to **dissented** as **agreed** is to _____
   a. glad   b. agree   c. greedy   d. disagreed

4. **converse** is to **conversation** as **starve** is to _____
   a. starvation   b. famine   c. diet   d. overeat
   Clue: This one has to do with parts of speech!

5. **efficiency** is to **efficient** as **deficiency** is to _____
   a. small   b. fish   c. deficient   d. fission

6. **fatigue** is to **exhaustion** as **happy** is to _____
   a. sad   b. glad   c. unhappy   d. sacred

7. **innovative** is to **new** as **uniform** is to _____
   a. different   b. unlike   c. alike   d. formula

8. **miscellaneous** is to **uniform** as **skeptics** is to _____
   a. believers   b. adults   c. doubters   d. doctors

9. **sturdy** is to **wordy** as **milk** is to _____
   a. silk   b. strong   c. sound   d. weak

10. **ordeal** is to **trial** as **labor** is to _____
    a. Labor Day   b. toil   c. laziness   d. sleep

Nonfiction ~ (Textbook p. 396)

Florence Nightingale

MORE ABOUT THE STORY
Writing Activity

The Crimean War

Look up the Crimean War in an encyclopedia. If you can, find information at the library as well.
(1) Give some facts about the war.
(2) Why were the British a part of this war?
(3) Do you think their reasons for joining the fight were good ones?
(4) How should a country treat its soldiers?

Name _____

Florence Nightingale

MORE ABOUT THE STORY

Writing Activity

Nonfiction ~ (Textbook p. 396)

Florence Nightingale

GRAPHIC ORGANIZER
Summarizing Elements of Plot

The Lady With the Lamp

In Crimea, Florence Nightingale encountered horrors beyond her imagination. She rolled up her sleeves and got to work improving conditions for the soldiers of the British army. The men dubbed her "the lady with the lamp," not only because she often worked through the dark nights by lamplight, but also because to the men, she herself was a light in the terrible darkness of war.

In the exercise below, there are five dark clouds representing five major obstacles Miss Nightingale encountered. On the lines below the diagram, describe, in a sentence or two, what she did to "light up" these dark clouds.

Nonfiction ~ (Textbook p. 396)

Name _____

Florence Nightingale

GRAPHIC ORGANIZER

Summarizing Elements of Plot

Ring Out the Old, Ring in the New

Florence Nightingale changed the way hospitals were operated. Although her advances were introduced to aid wounded soldiers near the battlefield, her improvements and changes were eventually adopted by hospitals everywhere.

In the exercise below, you will find a list of seven terrible conditions in the Crimean hospital that Florence Nightingale changed for the better. In the column entitled "Ring in the New," describe the changes made by Florence Nightingale.

Ring Out the Old	Ring In the New
1. There are no clean shirts. The men have only rags saturated with blood.	
2. ...underneath its imposing mass are sewers loaded with filth.	
3. ...even the commonest utensils for cleanliness, decency, and comfort are lacking.	
4. ...sometimes a patient got a lump entirely gristle, the next might be entirely fat or entirely bone.	
5. ...they regarded the soldiers as military machines.	
6. ...the soldiers had come to look upon themselves as mere machines...	
7. ...the new hospital was designed to reproduce all the worst faults of the outdated hospitals of the past.	

Nonfiction ~ (Textbook p. 396)

Morning—"The Bird Perched for Flight"

VOCABULARY
Activity 1

> diminishing   launching   perched   vanished   vulnerable
> furiously   monitoring   scattered   vapor

1. When Alice entered Wonderland, she drank from a bottle that said, "Drink Me." The result was that she _____ (decreased) in size. Clearly, she was _____ (capable of being physically or emotionally wounded) to the effects of the potion, because it acted quickly.

2. How did she get to Wonderland? She was following a large white rabbit who had _____ (disappeared) into a hole. While she was in Wonderland, she met many personalities. One, the Cheshire Cat, was _____ (rested on a high place) on the branch of a tree. He would disappear, but his smile remained.

3. Alice also met a very strange Queen, who was often _____ (very angry). My feeling is that the Queen's thoughts—and the subjects that she ruled—were very _____ (separated and going in many directions).

4. Had the Queen been exposed to strange _____ (steam, fog, gases)? Or had Alice? Wonderland was not so wonderful. In fact, it was like a frightening dream.

5. Lewis Carroll _____ (sent forth with force) poor Alice into a not-wonderful Wonderland. I suppose he did it so that he could stay at home himself, and _____ (keeping track of; observe) Alice's experiences. Not very kind of him. But he did give the world a fabulous and brilliant tale.

Nonfiction ~ (Textbook p. 406)

Morning—"The Bird Perched for Flight"

VOCABULARY Activity II

Finish the Sentence

Complete the sentence with the phrase that best fits the meaning of the vocabulary word in bold.

1. The ice cubes **diminished** in size
   a. as I placed them in the freezer.
   b. as they began to melt.
   c. as they grew larger.

2. Because I was **monitoring** the experiment,
   a. I was able to observe it and record the results.
   b. I was able to participate in it.
   c. I ate my lunch and ignored what was taking place.

3. Dan was **furious** with me, so
   a. he burst into laughter.
   b. he said he couldn't wait to see me again.
   c. he spoke very angrily.

4. The scissors had **vanished**,
   a. so I picked it up, and cut out the pattern.
   b. even though I looked all over the house for it.
   c. because I put it in the basket with my other sewing supplies.

5. Actually, my needles and thread were **scattered** across the table,
   a. so there was a mess to clean up.
   b. so there was no mess to clean up.
   c. and I quickly set the table for dinner.

6. Mom boiled the water, so that the **vapor** would
   a. freeze as hard as rocks.
   b. would enter my nostrils and help me breath.
   c. remain in the pot.

7. Because Mr. Poe has asthma, he is **vulnerable** to
   a. the effects of nice weather.
   b. problems with breathing.
   c. nothing.

8. My cockatoo likes to **perch**, so he
   a. lies on the bottom of his cage.
   b. doesn't talk to strangers.
   c. sits on his little swing.

9. Have you ever watched a rocket being **launched**?
   a. It just remains on the ground.
   b. It moves up into the air, and goes forth into space.
   c. Everybody just walks around it on the ground—it's not going anywhere!

Morning—"The Bird Perched for Flight"

MORE ABOUT THE STORY
Writing Activity

When you studied the poetry unit, you learned about haiku. Haiku have only three lines. The first line has only five syllables; the second line has seven syllables; and the third line returns to five syllables. Use words from poetic passages in *Morning—"The Bird Perched for Flight,"* and create a haiku.

Example: Ducks call from nearby
Inlets. A cabbage palm stands.
Black against the sky.

Name _____

Morning—"The Bird Perched for Flight"
MORE ABOUT THE STORY
Writing Activity

Nonfiction ~ (Textbook p. 406)

Morning—"The Bird Perched for Flight"

GRAPHIC ORGANIZER
Sensory Images

When we read a story for the first time, we notice, primarily, the plot. We want to know what is happening, and we race to finish the story to find out how it ends. If we read the story a second time, we may focus on the characterization. A third reading might lead us to notice setting and style. The process is something akin to observing a building. At first glance, one notices its height and size and perhaps its color. A second look will introduce us to its lines, some of the materials used, perhaps its grounds. Only after returning to the building several times might an observer notice the color of the mortar between the bricks, the type of roof the building has, or the angle at which the sun strikes it in the morning.

In *Morning—"The Bird Perched for Flight,"* our senses of sight and sound are appealed to. You may not have even noticed how many colors your mind conjured up as you read the story, but once you do notice, you will see that the story is like a series of color slides displayed one after another.

To complete the exercise below, follow the instructions on each page.

Sound

Find eight phrases in the story that describe a sound. The reader imagines hearing these sounds as a background to the visual images described.

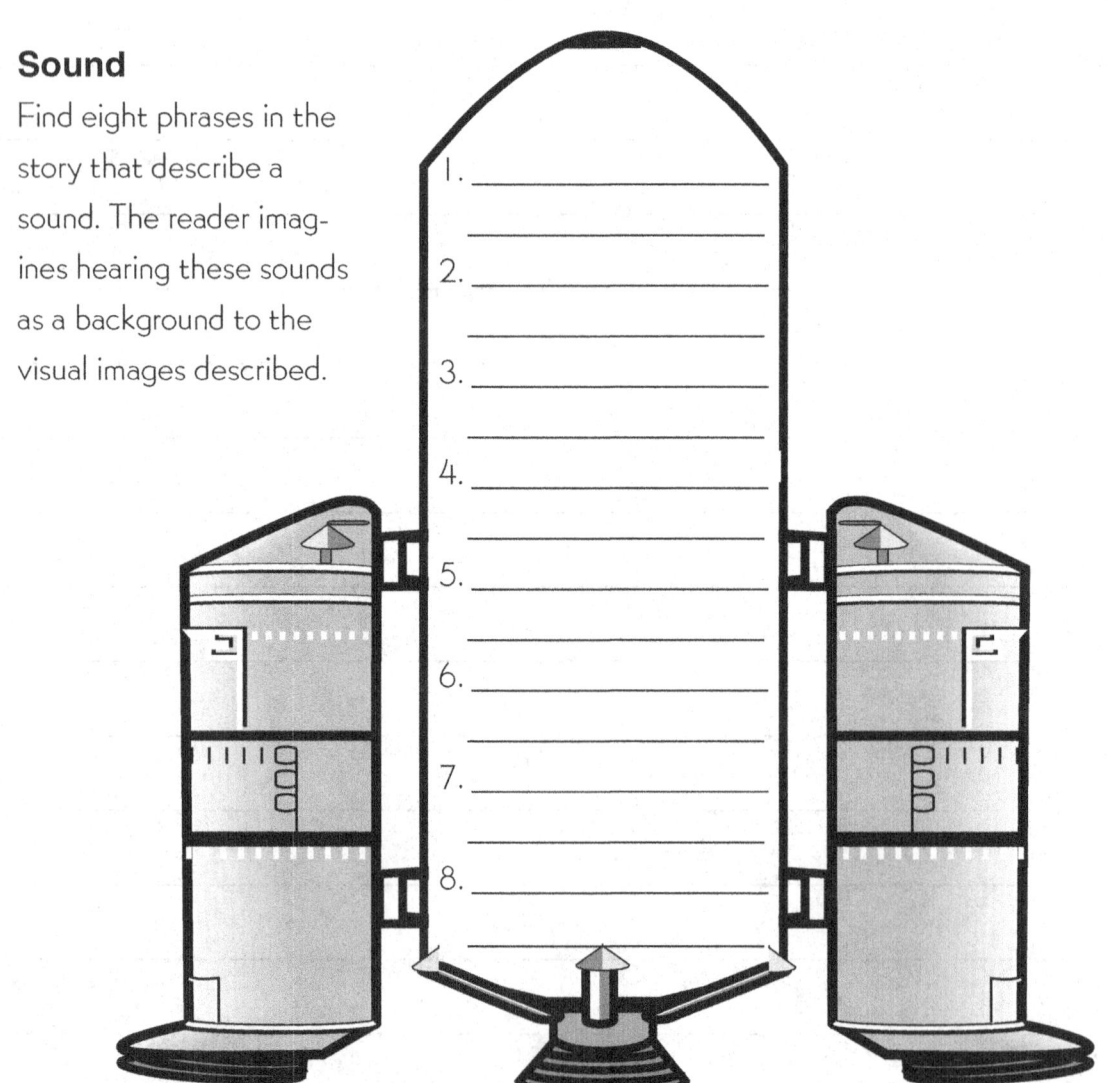

1. _____
2. _____
3. _____
4. _____
5. _____
6. _____
7. _____
8. _____

Nonfiction ~ (Textbook p. 406)

Name _____

Morning—"The Bird Perched for Flight"

GRAPHIC ORGANIZER

Sensory Images

Color

What colors do you envision upon reading the following phrases? Include both the color of the object described and the color of the background against which it is set.

	Object	Background
1. It is dark...with a sky full of stars.		
2. A cabbage palm stands up black against a shadowy sky		
3. As dawn flushes the horizon...		
4. It is still morning...		
5. Vapor trails...		
6. an almost cloudless sky		
7. the morning light		
8. Vapor steams furiously off its side		
9. A jet of steam shoots from the pad		
10. Now great flames spurt...		
11. Clouds of smoke billow...		
12. the rocket begins to rise		
13. the cloud of fire and smoke		
14. a great flock of ducks		
15. It is up and away, a comet boring through the sky		
16. it has made its own cloud—a huge vapor trail		
17. There, above the cloud now, reappears the rocket, only a very bright star		
18. A cloud of brown smoke hangs...		
19. It steams in the bright morning air		
20. Above us the white vapor trail of the rocket		

Rattlesnake Hunt

VOCABULARY — Activity 1

> *accumulated   camouflaged   desolate   immobility   portable*
> *arid   cautiously   forage   limply   translucent*

1. They thought that because the Kalahari Desert plateau is always so _____ (*excessively dry*), it had little plant or animal life. Simply put, without obvious sources of water, how could the plants or animals or insects live?

2. We moved out into the desert _____ (*carefully*) in the night. The plants, trees, and shadows _____ (*concealed*) us, but the moon was shining brightly. At one point, we heard noises, and I was frightened into _____ (*the state of being motionless*).

3. I remembered the advice I had received about working with Physicians Without Borders. Now, my _____ (*piled up*) fears seemed to take over. I was no longer so brave.

4. When morning came, I looked out over the _____ (*empty; deserted*) landscape. How could people live anywhere near here, especially with the war? How did animals _____ (*search for provisions or food*) for food?

5. Indeed, the place had a strange and silent beauty. Some of the cactus leaves were even _____ (*letting light shine through*).

6. Despite our need for haste, we had decided that it would be much safer if we took the _____ (*movable; easily carried*) radio. It was a two-way system, and would help us talk with a rescue party, if one were on the way.

7. We stopped briefly to eat. I wanted to ask John what our chances were. But he seemed so tired, I held back. His clothing and hair hung _____ (*drooping; lacking firmness*) in the terrible heat.

Pick the Synonym

Only one word is a synonym for the vocabulary word. Circle it.

1. **translucent**
   a. dark
   b. sunny
   c. lets light shine through

2. **desolate**
   a. crowded
   b. lonely
   c. cheerful

3. **arid**
   a. dry
   b. wet
   c. windy

4. **forage**
   a. forest
   b. porridge
   c. search for food

5. **limply**
   a. stiffly
   b. drooping
   c. strongly

6. **accumulated**
   a. collected
   b. scattered
   c. threw away

7. **portable**
   a. affordable
   b. movable
   c. immovable

8. **camouflaged**
   a. disguised
   b. exposed
   c. carried

9. **immobility**
   a. motion
   b. mobility
   c. inability to move

10. **cautiously**
    a. daringly
    b. carefully
    c. foolishly

Rattlesnake Hunt

MORE ABOUT THE STORY
Writing Activity

> Often, when we are afraid of something—insects, mice, snakes, or even dogs and cats—it's hard to admit to others that we are afraid. It's hard to say, "I'm afraid of _____." We don't feel that it is our personal job to be courageous, and to work on our fears. Why is that? For this exercise,
>
> (1) Pick one thing you are afraid of, and name it, in one sentence.
>
> (2) Write down what it is that frightens you. Don't answer, "I don't know why." Don't say, "I am afraid of snakes, because snakes are—" Write, instead, "I am afraid of snakes, because I worry that..." Take responsibility for your fear.
>
> (3) Why is it important to work on overcoming our fears?

Name _____

Rattlesnake Hunt

MORE ABOUT THE STORY
Writing Activity

Nonfiction ~ (Textbook p. 412)

Rattlesnake Hunt

GRAPHIC ORGANIZER
Distilling Facts

"It is difficult to be afraid of anything about which enough is known."

Although one learns many facts about rattlesnakes from this story, the lesson of the story is more important than each of those facts. The lesson is that we can conquer our fears and diminish our anxiety about anything in life by learning more about what frightens us. The more informed we are, the less fearful we are.

In the exercise below, you will find seven fears that the author had about snakes. At the end of the "fears" you will find a list of facts about snakes that, once learned, calmed the author's fears. Choosing from the list of facts, write a "herpetology fact" that would best calm the stated fear.

Fear	Fear
1. How can we hunt for snakes when we have no idea where they live? Why, we might come across one anywhere!	2. When do they come out of their holes? I'm afraid all the time!
Fact	**Fact**

Fear	Fear
3. I've heard snakes like the heat. Is this true? Should I stay away from this area during the hottest part of the summer?	4. Well, perhaps they like cool weather. I'm afraid they're zipping around all over because it's nice and cool. *Get me out of here!*
Fact	**Fact**

Nonfiction ~ (Textbook p. 412)

Rattlesnake Hunt

Name _____

GRAPHIC ORGANIZER
Distilling Facts

Fear	Fear
5. If I see a rattler, should I run? I'm afraid my knees will turn to jelly!	6. I heard that if you see a rattler you should let it know you've seen him and try to scare him off. But I'm afraid I'd be so scared I'd be paralyzed with fear!
Fact	**Fact**
_____	_____

Fear	
7. Do snakes have good eyes? I'll bet they can hit a target at fifteen feet! HELP!	
Fact	
_____	

Choose from these Herpetology Facts
1. When the weather is cool, snakes are sluggish.
2. A rattler will lie quietly without revealing itself if a man passes by and it thinks it is not seen.
3. Snakes live in gopher holes in the winter.
4. Rattlers pay no attention to a man standing perfectly still.
5. Snakes can't stand too much heat.
6. They come out in the midday warmth.
7. When the weather is cool snakes are sluggish.

Nonfiction ~ (Textbook p. 412)

Beneath the Crags of Malpelo Island

VOCABULARY

Activity 1

abruptly   descent   jutted   punctured   writhing
deflating   jerked   perished   tarpaulin

1. The trip in the air balloon was exciting and scary. Jerry held his breath as the balloon rose. The view of the land below was thrilling. If someone had asked him, he might even have said that it was spectacular! He knew that their _____ (*proceeding from high to low*) would not begin until the captain started _____ (*releasing air*) the huge balloon above them.

2. Their food and supplies were protected from rain and snow by a red _____ (*waterproof material used for protection*). The three boys sat at the captain's instructions. Jerry thought the captain looked worried.

3. _____ (*unexpectedly*), the air balloon _____ (*pulled suddenly*)! They flew closer to the mountain than he had expected they would. Jerry felt as though he could reach out and touch the big boulders that _____ (*extended*) out from Mt. Helen.

4. He heard a loud hiss. Had the balloon been _____ (*pierced*)? Maybe this trip wasn't such a good idea.

5. His stomach hurt. He felt as if snakes were _____ (*twisting*) in his belly. He tried to focus on the forest below them. But all he could feel was cold fear.

6. Jason looked over at him. "Hey, Jerry!" he shouted into the wind. "Are you okay?" "Sure, sure," Jerry yelled back. Jason reached over and grabbed Jerry's hand. "I'm telling you, Jerr, you look green. Hey, we're okay. It's always like this. We're doing fine." Jerry felt relief. "You mean we're not going to _____ (*die*)?" Jason smiled. "I love you, little brother. I love your big vocabulary and your big heart. We're doing great. Enjoy the ride." And you know what? He did.

Nonfiction ~ (Textbook p. 420)

Name _____

Beneath the Crags of Malpelo Island

VOCABULARY
Activity 11

Create Your Own Crossword

For this first try at making a crossword, you don't have to write the Across and Down clues. Just write in words where they work. Make sure you don't end up with any letters next to each other—either Across or Down—that aren't complete words.

Crossword #1

	D	E	F	L	A	T	I	N	G	
		E			B					
		S			R					
		C			U					
		E			P					
		N			T					
		T			L					
					Y					

Crossword #2

			W			
	J	E	R	K	E	D
	U		I			
	T		T			
	T		H			
	E		I			
	D		N			
			G			

Crossword #3

	P	E	R	I	S	H	E	D	
	U								
	N								
	C								
	T	A	R	P	A	U	L	I	N
	U								
	R								
	E								
	D								

Nonfiction ~ (Textbook p. 420)   199

Beneath the Crags of Malpelo Island

MORE ABOUT THE STORY
Writing Activity

> It's time to find out about octopi—that's plural for octopus. Read and get the facts. Look for basic information, and find out whether an octopus is likely to be aggressive. Think about the rattlesnake story, where we learned that rattlesnakes actually try to *avoid* human beings.
>
> Harry Earl Rieseberg says his octopus is a "monster," "a terrible creature" with "devilish eyes." On page 427, he says the octopus seemed to realize what his intent was. Is an octopus capable of thinking? He also describes the octopus as "enraged" and "desperate." Does an octopus feel anger and despair?
>
> This is your chance to be a naturalist. After you read about octopi, write down all the words and phrases that Rieseberg uses that show how he, himself, feels—but that really have nothing to do with the nature of the octopus.

Name _____

Beneath the Crags of Malpelo Island

MORE ABOUT THE STORY

Writing Activity

Nonfiction ~ (Textbook p. 420)

Beneath the Crags of Malpelo Island

GRAPHIC ORGANIZER
Outlining One Element of Plot

Would you want to dive for treasure deep down into the bottom of the sea? You would have to be pretty fearless to do so! Harry Rieseberg describes the many frightening things he could have or actually did encounter while diving near Malpelo Island. In the chart below, write one scary event or object that Harry tells of in this harrowing story, in each of the boxes. You may include some events that he took precautions against but which he did not actually experience.

Exercise One

1. Sharks could attack.

2. _____

3. _____

4. _____

5. _____

6. _____

7. _____

8. _____

Nonfiction ~ (Textbook p. 420)

Name _____

Beneath the Crags of Malpelo Island

GRAPHIC ORGANIZER

Outlining One Element of Plot

In Exercise One, you listed eight scary events or things that Harry had to fear. Harry was a professional, and did not face dangerous or frightening things without preparing for them. However, some of the events were so unexpected that he could not have prepared for them. Choose five of the dangers you listed in the chart on the previous page. Now, go back to the story and discover what Harry did to prepare for those dangers. Write one answer in each bubble. Mark by number on the designated line which danger you are writing about.

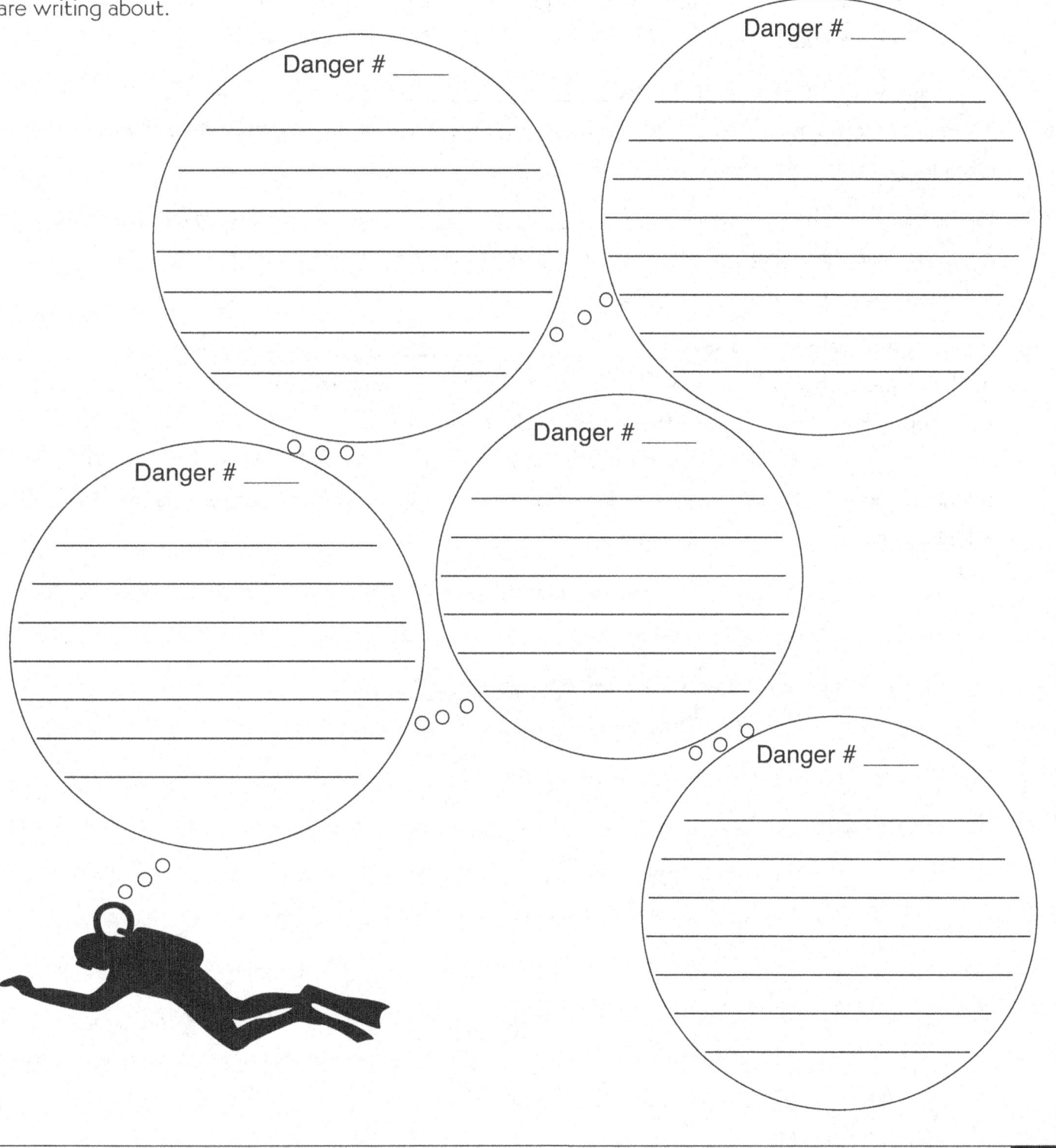

Nonfiction ~ (Textbook p. 420)   203

Penicillin and Company

VOCABULARY
Activity 1

microbes   specimen   strep   spore

1. Has your throat ever hurt so much that it seemed like you couldn't swallow? Ten percent of all sore throats are _____ *(an abbreviation of streptococcus, a disease-causing bacteria)* throat. This is a disease caused by tiny egg-shaped bacteria, called Group A streptococci (strep-toe-cock-eye).

2. Anywhere you find water, you will find _____ *(very small disease-causing bacteria or organisms)*. Like other living creatures, these microscopic organisms require water in order to live and to reproduce.

3. Plants that don't flower produce _____s *(a simple, one-celled organism produced by plants, fungi, and other microorganisms)*. This is the way that ferns, mosses, and mushrooms create more ferns, mosses, and mushrooms.

4. An interesting activity is to save leaf _____ *(samples)*. Take a telephone book outside with you. When you find leaf samples that you want to save for your collection, just snip them off the tree and place them in your telephone book. Later, when you return home, you can store your telephone book in a warm, dry spot for several days. Put a heavy book on top of the telephone book, so that your leaves will dry flat. Don't forget to remove your leaves and put the telephone book back where it belongs.

Drama ~ (Textbook p. 434)

Translating Secret Code

Here is your secret code:

A = T	H = B	O = D	V = O
B = Q	I = H	P = X	W = N
C = W	J = U	Q = F	X = K
D = A	K = V	R = I	Y = S
E = L	L = C	S = Y	Z = J
F = R	M = E	T = G	
G = M	N = Z	U = P	

Now translate each code word into a vocabulary word. For example, if you were translating the word *chicken*, it would appear as W B H W V L Z, simply by substituting the code letters for the usual letters.

grlfvhmy   M I C R O B E S

yumlrgmw   S P E C I M E N

yafmu   S T R E P

yuvfm   S P O R E

Penicillin and Company

MORE ABOUT THE STORY
Writing Activity

What is an *antibiotic*? Where does the word come from? What is a good definition of the term?

Write down the etymology (the history of the word) of *antibiotic* and an accurate definition that you, yourself, understand. Then do some research, and write a paragraph on some fact about antibiotics that you find interesting.

Drama ~ (Textbook p. 434)

Name _____

Penicillin and Company
MORE ABOUT THE STORY
Writing Activity

Penicillin and Company

GRAPHIC ORGANIZER
Comprehension Check

Penicillin was discovered in three stages. Complete the diagram by filling in the missing information on the lines provided.

1. Dr. Fleming was studying _____.
2. He discovered that they were being killed by _____.
3. He tested them and found they killed germs that caused the diseases _____, _____, and _____.
4. He tested penicillin first on _____ _____ _____, second on _____, and finally on a _____ _____.
5. He discovered that penicillin was harmless to _____ _____.
6. But he ran into a problem. It was _____ _____.

1. Drs. Florey and Chain began to study penicillin _____ years later.
2. Their goal was to turn it into an _____ so that it could be _____.
3. They found a policeman who was infected with _____.
4. When they treated him, his condition _____.
5. But they ran into a problem—it was _____ _____ _____.

Drama ~ (Textbook p. 434)

Name _____

Penicillin and Company
GRAPHIC ORGANIZER
Comprehension Check

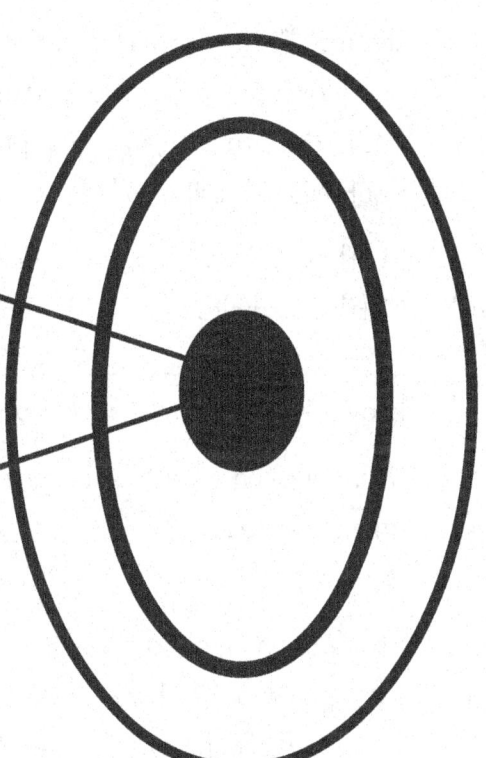

1. Dr. Florey arrived in the U.S. five months before _____ _____.
2. The Americans asked if penicillin could _____ _____ _____ _____.
3. The answer was _____.
4. Research was done in _____ _____ and _____.
5. Victory! Penicillin is produced!

Drama ~ (Textbook p. 434)   209

Grandpa and the Statue

VOCABULARY
Activity 1

engineered   pedestal   peeved   register   swindle

1. "Today," Ben's teacher declared, "we will learn about idioms." "What's an idiom?" Ben cried. His teacher said, "Ben, please. Please learn to raise your hand." Ben mumbled an apology. Ms. Kaufman paused. "An idiom is a phrase of two or more words that, together, have a different meaning from what the words literally mean." Several students shook their heads in confusion. "Let me give you an example. Here's an idiom. When a person comes from a family that is wealthy, people say that the person was *born with a silver spoon in his or her mouth*. Now, the baby certainly didn't come into the world with a spoon of any kind in its mouth. So it's an expression that is not literally true." Ben shouted, "Ms. Kaufman! Ms. Kaufman!" Ms. Kaufman smiled and said, "Ben, please. We have subjects we must cover today. No matter how you try to _____ (*plan; design or produce*) the situation, we must proceed." Ben's feelings were hurt, but he *put on a brave face*. Ms. Kaufman didn't like to be so gruff, but she felt that *the ends justified the means*.

2. Matthew joked, "Ben, if you don't control yourself, Ms. Kaufman is going to *give us a hard time*." Matthew admired his teacher. She was the best one he'd ever had. He really *put her on a* _____ (*the base of an upright structure*). He continued, "Besides, Ben, you know Ms. Kaufman's *bark is worse than her bite*."

3. "Ms. Kaufman," Keith complained. "I don't want to be a *wet blanket*, but I *haven't got a clue* regarding idioms. I'm really _____ (*annoyed*). It *beats me* how anyone can understand what *literally* means."

4. Ms. Kaufman looked in her _____ (*a written record of names*) to see who was speaking. Keith was one of several new students, and she didn't know all of their names yet. She loved teaching, but sometimes she felt like she was *in over her head*.

5. "Boys, boys. It seems to me we are working *at cross purposes*. *At all costs*, you must try to understand idioms. If you do, you will be *ahead of the game*. If you don't, you'll never *cut the mustard*. Here's another example of an idiom. Let's say someone's trying to cheat you and make you a victim of a _____ (*deceitful trick*). There's an idiom to describe that. The expression for such a trick is a *confidence game*." She laughed. "Well, it's a good thing you are a *captive audience*—otherwise I might never get to explain this to you!"

The italicized phrases above are all idioms. You can look them up in an idiom dictionary or ask your teacher, if you don't know what they mean.

Name _____

Grandpa and the Statue

VOCABULARY

Activity 11

I'm Thinking of a Word

1. I'm thinking of a word that is 6 letters long and means *fretful, ill-tempered,* or *annoyed*. That word is

   ___ ___ ___ ___ ___ ___ .

2. I'm thinking of a word that is 8 letters long and means *base, foundation,* or *stand*. That word is

   ___ ___ ___ ___ ___ ___ ___ ___ .

3. I'm thinking of a word that is 8 letters long and means *a written record containing regular entries*. That word is

   ___ ___ ___ ___ ___ ___ ___ ___ .

4. I'm thinking of a word that is 8 letters long and means *contrive, plan, or guide the course of*. That word is

   ___ ___ ___ ___ ___ ___ ___ ___ .

5. I'm thinking of a word that is 7 letters long and means *an instance of obtaining money or property by fraud or deceit*. That word is

   ___ ___ ___ ___ ___ ___ ___ .

Drama ~ (Textbook p. 444)

Grandpa and the Statue

MORE ABOUT THE STORY
Writing Activity

On page 455 in the textbook, Monaghan reads from the Emma Lazarus poem, *The New Colossus*, that is on the Statue of Liberty. Now, officials have selected *you* to write a short poem or prose paragraph for the statue. Your work will replace Ms. Lazarus's poem. What do you write?

Name _____

Grandpa and the Statue

MORE ABOUT THE STORY

Writing Activity

Drama ~ (Textbook p. 444)

Grandpa and the Statue

GRAPHIC ORGANIZER
Reading Drama

A Play Within a Play

Grandpa and the Statue is actually two plays, not one. The first, or outer, play is about a wounded war veteran by the name of Monaghan. The second, or inner, play is the story of a little boy and his grandfather. The second play explains and gives meaning to the first play. But the structure of story does not end here. At the center of the two plays stands the Statue of Liberty and what it symbolizes. Arthur Miller wrote his "play within a play" to explain what the Statue of Liberty means to Americans and to all those who yearn to become Americans.

In the diagram on the opposite page, you see an outer frame, signifying the outer play; the inner frame, signifying the inner play; and the central box with a picture of the Statue of Liberty in it. On this page, you will find questions on each of the three parts of the play. Write the answers to each question in the appropriate box of the diagram.

Questions on the "outer play"
1. Describe what the audience sees on stage as the curtains open.
2. What happened to Monaghan?
3. Which war do you think Monaghan fought in? On what are you basing your opinion?
4. Monaghan says "I'm not blue." Based on your reading of the play, do you think this is true? Support your opinion.

Questions on the "inner play" (to be answered in the middle frame)
1. What are two of Old Monaghan's objections to the Statue of Liberty?
2. What message does Old Monaghan insist should have been written on the statue?
3. The veteran that Old Monaghan meets at the Statue of Liberty shows him that each of his objections or predictions is unfounded. How does the veteran dispel each of the following:
    a. the statue's swaying proves it will soon collapse
    b. nobody really cares about the statue
    c. the statue has no meaning for an American
4. What becomes of Gramps' insistence that the statue need say no more than "Welcome"? Does he change his mind?

The meaning of the Statue of Liberty
1. Explain why the wounded Monaghan looks out at the Statue of Liberty so often.

Grandpa and the Statue

GRAPHIC ORGANIZER

Reading Drama

Name _____

1. _____

   1. _____

      1. _____

      2. _____

   2. _____

   3. _____

2. _____

3. _____

4. _____

Drama ~ (Textbook p. 444) 215

The Voyages of Dr. Dolittle
Part One

VOCABULARY
Activity 1

annoyance	chattered	impatiently	surgeon
antics	cobbler	incessantly	tiresome
anxious	gravely	solitary	voyages

1. My mother worked as a _____ (*doctor who is expert at performing operations*) in a big city hospital. She told me that when she was growing up, she had to decide whether she wanted to be a doctor, or whether she wanted to be a _____ (*shoemaker*). Of course, this was a very difficult decision for her, because both occupations seemed *very* interesting.

2. She did admit to us that always, before performing an operation, she would try to relax. Otherwise, she felt too _____ (*concerned; worried*), and she certainly did not want to communicate that to her patients or their family members. We discussed this in her later years, after she had retired, and she talked about it _____ (*seriously*). Mother was never one to _____ (*talk idly and incessantly*).

3. In fact, when other people talked _____ (*without ceasing; with repetition*), I know she found them rather _____ (*annoying*), although of course she would never have said so.

4. I loved my mother. She was just the perfect person. I am very fortunate. We had wonderful times together. When she was seventy, she decided it was time to see the world. We traveled the globe together, because she wanted me to be her companion on all of her _____ (*journeys, especially those taken by sea*). I will never forget those times.

5. Greta reacted to her brother's _____ (*attention-drawing, often wildly playful or funny, acts or actions; jokes, tricks*) with irritation. "Gary," she said _____ (*restlessly; in a manner that is without patience*), "can't you grow up and act your age?"

6. Gary, of course, responded with _____ (*irritation*). "Greta!" he exclaimed. "Do you have to be bothered by every single _____ (*alone; without companions*) thing that I do? Can't a person just have fun?" Then Greta felt bad, and wondered to herself why she was always critical of him. "I'm sorry, Gary. I'm really sorry." But would she be able to be nicer in the future? What was the point of saying sorry, if she were to be mean to her brother again? He was really a good boy.

Name _____

The Voyages of Dr. Dolittle
Part One
VOCABULARY
Activity II

Filling in Crossword Across and Down Clues

Now it's your turn to fill in the Across and Down clues, using definitions or synonyms for the word that already appears in the crossword puzzle. Check the Across or Down number when you write your clue. If you need help, look up the word in the dictionary. Two letters together that aren't a word may be an abbreviation, which you'll also find in the dictionary.

Crossword grid entries:
- 1 Across: TO
- 6 Across: INCESSANTLY
- 8 Across: INCH
- 9 Across: SEA
- 11 Across: INK
- 13 Across: TIRESOME
- 17 Across: TEAM
- 18 Across: ME
- 19 Across: SURGEON
- 21 Across: EWE
- 24 Across: ORDER
- 26 Across: VOYAGE

Down entries:
- 1: T, I, N, S, T
- 2: O
- 3: U, E
- 4: A, X, A, V, S
- 5: F, L, A, E, S
- 7: C
- 10: G
- 12: K
- 14: I
- 15: S
- 16: B, E, E
- 20: N
- 22: W
- 23: E
- 25: R

Across
1. _____
6. _____
8. _____
9. _____
11. _____
13. _____
17. _____
18. _____
19. _____
21. _____
24. _____
26. _____

Down
1. _____
2. _____
3. _____
4. _____
5. _____
7. _____
10. _____
12. _____
14. _____
15. _____
16. _____
20. _____
21. _____
22. _____
23. _____
25. _____

The Novel ~ (Textbook p. 460)

The Voyages of Dr. Dolittle Part One

MORE ABOUT THE STORY
Writing Activity

> What is Colonel Bellowes thinking about when he is out for his walk? Write his thoughts in the Colonel's voice, using the pronoun *I*. See pages 467-468 in the textbook, to help you with his character.

Name _____

**The Voyages of Dr. Dolittle
Part One**

MORE ABOUT THE STORY

Writing Activity

The Novel ~ (Textbook p. 460)

The Voyages of Dr. Dolittle
Part One

GRAPHIC ORGANIZER
Bringing a Story to Life

In a few short pages, we are introduced to an entire menagerie of animals, birds, and fish. Did you recognize each one? Imagine that you were preparing a glossary for the story. Make a list of every creature mentioned in the story (including the seafood Joe sells) and alphabetize it.

1.	4.	7.	10.
2.	5.	8.	11.
3.	6.	9.	12. Wiff-Waff

Now that you have alphabetized the twelve creatures' names (including the imaginary Wiff-Waff), list them in the left hand column of the chart below. In the next column, draw or trace small pictures of the creature. In the next column, write the word we use for the sound the animal makes (e.g. a lion roars, a dog barks, etc.). If the creature does not make a sound, put a large dash in the column. If you do not know the name for the sound the creature makes, make one up and put a star next to it. In the last column, write the word for the group of the animal, bird, or fish. You will be surprised to find that there is a specific word for many animal groups. Below the chart, we have listed the names of the groups of some of the animals in the chart. If you do not recognize them, guess which creature they go with. The answers are printed upside down at the end of the page. (For the Wiff-Waff, you may make up the answers and the illustration.)

Creature	Illustration	Sound	Group Term

The Novel ~ (Textbook p. 460)

The Voyages of Dr. Dolittle Part One

GRAPHIC ORGANIZER
Bringing a Story to Life

Name _____

Creature	Illustration	Sound	Group Term

| a brace | a pack | a flock | a kit |
| a pandemonium | a flight | a parliament | a cete |

A cete of badgers; a flight of doves; a brace of ducks; a flock of lambs; a parliament of owls; a pandemonium of parrots; a kit of pigeons (all flying together); a pack of rats.

The Novel ~ (Textbook p. 460)

The Voyages of Dr. Dolittle
Part Two

VOCABULARY
Activity 1

biased	eminent	hamper	philosopher	sketch
despised	frowned	impertinent	rattle	solemn
dismally	gasp	lingered	scrambled	stern

1. There I was, raiding the refrigerator in the middle of the night, when the glass containers on the top shelf _____ (*made a rapid succession of short sharp noises; moved or shook with a clatter*)! Mom, who is a very light sleeper, shouted from her bed, "So who's the thief?" "Mom...It's me!" I shouted, embarrassed. As hungry as I was, I was *not* going to _____ (*be slow in parting, hang around*). I _____ (*hurried, moved with urgency*) for the stairs.

2. I never fib to Mom. Mom's wonderful. She is _____ (*strict*) about mealtimes, because she leaves for her job early each morning, and she wants to have dinner on the table when Dad gets home each night. She _____ (*looks down on; hates*) our eating food she has prepared for the next day without our asking.

3. Thinking about that, I realized I had behaved _____ (*miserably*). As I climbed the stairs, I could picture Mom _____ (*looking displeased*) and _____ (*serious*). How could I make up for it? I hadn't really thought about it carefully. I just was hungry. I hadn't wanted to _____ (*interfere with*) the smooth progress of our family life!

4. Mom always described Dad as an _____ (*outstanding, prominent*) person and father. Some people might think her _____ (*prejudiced*), but all of us kids agreed. To give you some idea—a verbal _____ (*rough drawing*)— I should tell you that he is very good-hearted and generous, and a bit of a _____ (*one who studies ideas and seeks wisdom*).

5. He always gives people the benefit of the doubt. I have never, ever seen him behave _____ (*rudely*). As I got under the covers, I thought about how good it feels when he gives me a hug. And then I woke up! I _____ (*caught my breath with shock*) with relief. It had only been a dream.

The Novel ~ (Textbook p. 500)

Name _____

The Voyages of Dr. Dolittle
Part Two
VOCABULARY
Activity II

True or False?

Circle the correct answer.

1. If ideas are **not** important to you, you are a **philosopher**.   T or F

2. My aunts and uncles had lots of fun. It was a **solemn** occasion.   T or F

3. Shirley **frowned**, because she was displeased.   T or F

4. The police were in a hurry, and **scrambled** to get inside.   T or F

5. Dave spoke rudely, and Ms. Hewitt said he was **impertinent**.   T or F

6. A map needs to be very precise—like a **sketch**!   T or F

7. It's clear that Capt. Doherty dislikes people of color. I'm
   surprised that he's so **biased**.   T or F

8. In Los Angeles, the freeways are so crowded, our progress
   was **hampered** at all hours of the day.   T or F

9. Oh, he's nobody! That's why he's so **eminent**!   T or F

10. Dirk was so surprised when he opened the door, he **gasped**.   T or F

11. The boys moved so quickly, they were accused of **lingering**.   T or F

12. Because of the sound its tail makes, it's called a **rattle**snake.   T or F

13. I love listening to Mozart. That's why I **despise** his music.   T or F

14. Edward was **stern**. There was a hardness or severity to his manner.   T or F

15. "I'm so happy. So carefree. So looking forward to being home,"
    Maria said **dismally**.   T or F

The Novel ~ (Textbook p. 500)

The Voyages of Dr. Dolittle
Part Two
MORE ABOUT THE STORY
Writing Activity

One of the great pleasures of reading *The Voyages of Dr. Dolittle* is the hopefulness and happiness that are threaded throughout the story. A good example is the outcome of Luke's trial and the cheering of the townsfolk that follows. Describe a happy story you recently heard on the news, read in a newspaper, or overheard your parents discussing. If you haven't heard of anything good happening in the world lately, write about something good—a world event—that you *wish* you had heard about.

Name _____

**The Voyages of Dr. Dolittle
Part Two**

MORE ABOUT THE STORY

Writing Activity

The Voyages of Dr. Dolittle
Part Two

GRAPHIC ORGANIZER

Understanding Characters

The first section of Part Two describes an English courtroom. In each of the boxes drawn below, one courtroom figure is named. Answer the questions about him on the lines provided.

1. **The Judge**
   What is his name? _____
   What is his title? _____
   What is he wearing? _____

2. **The Jury**
   How many members are there? _____
   What is their job? _____

3. **The Policeman**
   How many are there? _____
   What is their job? _____
   Who "invented" their job? _____

4. **The Defendant**
   What is his name? _____
   What does he look like? _____

5. **The Defense Attorney**
   What is his name? _____
   What does he look like? _____

6. **The Prosecutor**
   What is his name? _____
   What does he look like? _____

7. **The Witness: Bob**
   What does he look like? _____
   What character traits does he display throughout? _____

8. **The Expert Witness: Dr. Dolittle**
   What character traits does he display after the trial? _____

226   The Novel ~ (Textbook p. 500)

Name _____

The Voyages of Dr. Dolittle Part Two

GRAPHIC ORGANIZER

Understanding Characters

Before you is a map of the Eastern Hemisphere. Play a game of "Blind Travel"! Close your eyes and place the point of your pencil on the map. Open your eyes and circle the place you touched. Look up the place in an atlas or encyclopedia and learn more about its climate and environment. Now, imagine you were going with Dr. Dolittle and Tommy Stubbins on a voyage to this place. Basing your choices on what you have learned, write a list of what you would take along and why you would take those particular items.

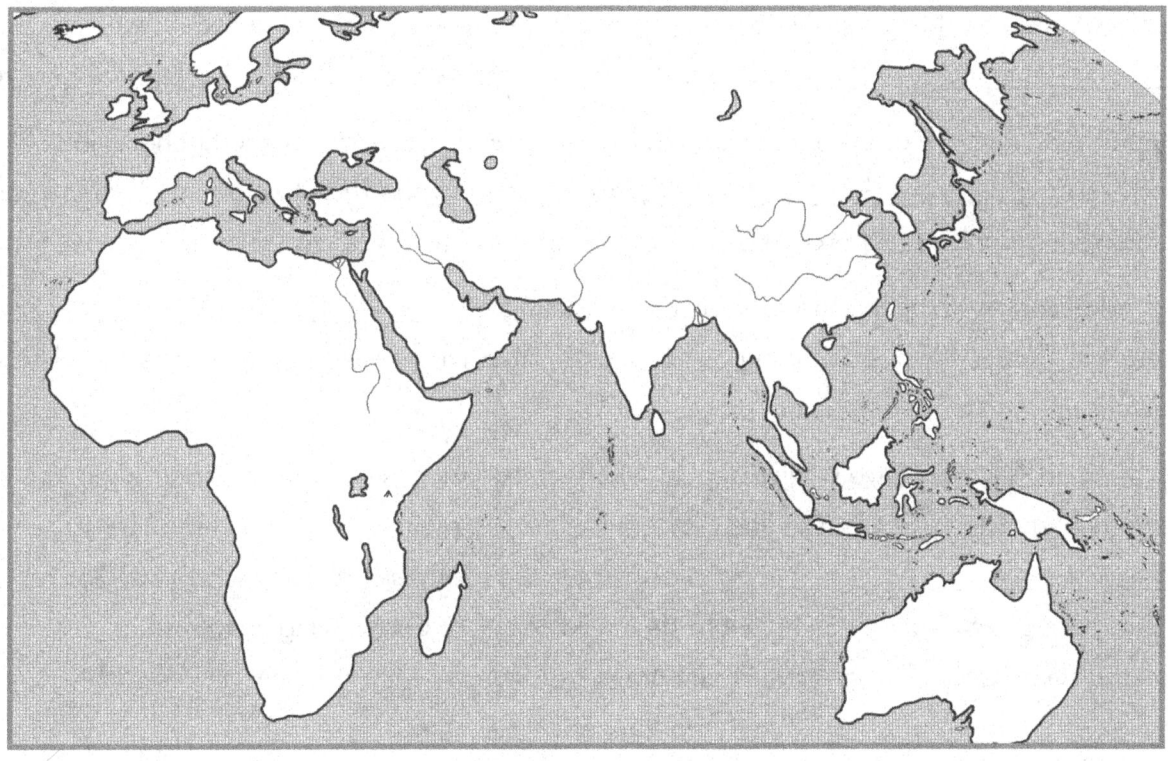

_____
_____
_____
_____
_____
_____
_____
_____
_____
_____
_____
_____
_____

The Novel ~ (Textbook p. 500)

The Voyages of Dr. Dolittle
Part Three

VOCABULARY
Activity 1

| colossal | hospitable | procession | racket | sufficient |
| cowardly | implored | provisions | simultaneous | venturesome |

1. My father had a serious look on his face. "Young man, we have something to discuss." "Oh Dad," I said, my voice trembling. I stopped in my tracks. "When you say that, I feel so _____ (not bravely)." My father patted me on the back to reassure me.

2. My mother had made us both a cup of tea. My father and I sat down at the kitchen table. Mom is always so _____ (giving a generous and friendly welcome) when I come home from school, or Dad takes a break from his studies—as if we were honored guests.

3. My father took a sip of tea and said, "Jim, your room is a _____ (of very great size) mess." He placed his cup in the saucer. "Your mother and I would appreciate if you would clean it up."

4. "Dad," I said, "I know I have trouble seeing what you and Mom see. I love my room. And you know how my friends love it!" Mom smiled. "Of course, we are pleased that you have a constant _____ (a group of individuals moving along in an orderly way) of visitors. But have you ever worried that there might be a wild animal or two moving about under cover of the laundry, blankets, books, and toys? Sometimes, we wonder what it is that makes such a _____ (confused loud noise) up there."

5. I didn't want to let myself laugh. My parents can be very funny. "Dad, I am embarrassed that you had to ask." Dad bit into a cookie. "Jim, you're a good boy. I assume that this conversation will be _____ (enough) to bring about a change."

6. He took another sip of tea. "You're such a _____ (daring; adventurous) lad. Why not pretend your room is a jungle, or land that needs to be cleared? Think of yourself as an explorer or someone on safari, who simply must organize his _____ (supplies)!" _____ (occurring at the same time as) with his remarks, my mother burst into laughter.

7. I vowed to turn over a new leaf. But I have to confess that when I went upstairs, as I passed my sister's open door, I _____ (begged) her to help me do the job. "Look, Bethy. I'll give you my allowance for the next two weeks." "Oh Jimmy!" she exclaimed. "What would Mom and Dad say about *that*?"

The Novel ~ (Textbook p. 528)

Name _____

The Voyages of Dr. Dolittle Part Three
VOCABULARY
Activity 11

Mixed-Up Moby

Moby thinks words mean their opposite. Help Moby by filling in the blanks below. Make certain you use a dictionary in addition to the textbook.

1. **Racket** means silence! It really means _____.

2. The general declared, "We want all our soldiers to be **cowardly**." Why is he wrong? Cowardly means _____.

3. When someone is cowardly, they are also **venturesome**. Is that true? Venturesome means _____.

4. I ate dinner at 6:00 and Jeff ate at 8:00. Our meals were eaten **simultaneously**. Wrong! Simultaneous means _____.

5. Look at that ant on the pavement. Why, it's **colossal**! Wrong again. Don't you know that colossal means _____?

6. My next-door neighbor is not very welcoming. That's why I say that he's so **hospitable**. No, no! Hospitable means _____.

7. No one came. So Jane said that there was a **procession** of people. Why is Jane wrong? Procession means _____.

8. The campers had no supplies but lots of **provisions**. That doesn't make sense. Provisions means _____.

9. The gas tank was empty. Jed said, "That's **sufficient** for our trip." Tell Jed that sufficient means _____.

10. When someone gives you what you want without your asking, you have to **implore** them. Huh? Implore means _____.

The Novel ~ (Textbook p. 528)

The Voyages of Dr. Dolittle
Part Three
MORE ABOUT THE STORY
Writing Activity

> What is a curlew? Write out the definition, and then write a short story of several paragraphs with a curlew as the central character.

Name _____

**The Voyages of Dr. Dolittle
Part Three**

MORE ABOUT THE STORY

Writing Activity

The Novel ~ (Textbook p. 528)

The Voyages of Dr. Dolittle
Part Three

GRAPHIC ORGANIZER
Problem Solving

Have you ever played one of those arcade games where little puppets pop up and you must bang them down with a mallet? No sooner are those puppets down than others pop up. The object of the game is to bang them all down, but it's rough going! The problems in *The Voyages of Dr. Dolittle* are something like that game. They keep popping up and being solved, only for new ones to pop up.

In the diagram below, the problems that occur in Part Three of *The Voyages of Dr. Dolittle* are inside the ten puppets. How is each problem solved? Write the solutions into the mallets.

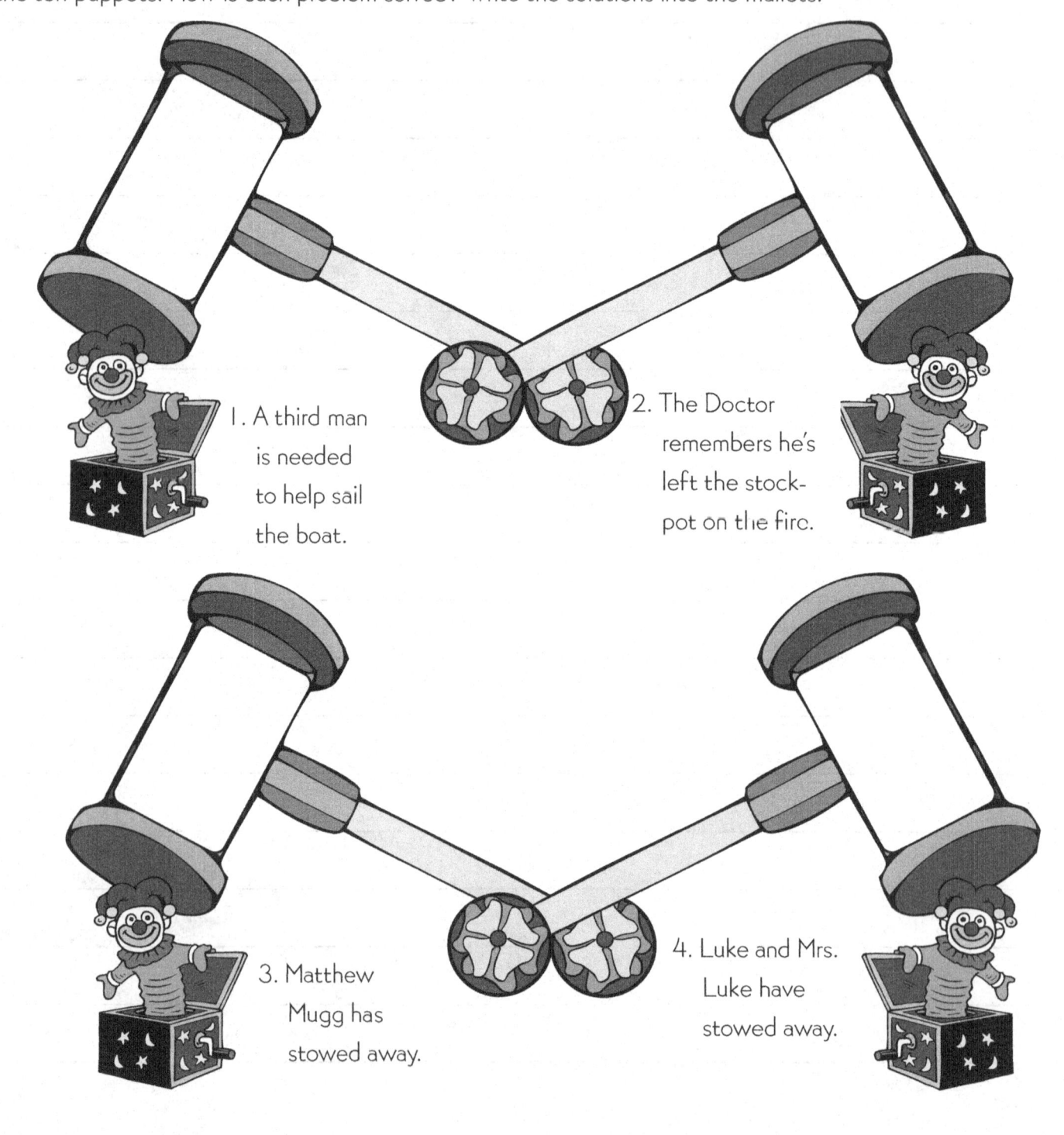

1. A third man is needed to help sail the boat.
2. The Doctor remembers he's left the stockpot on the fire.
3. Matthew Mugg has stowed away.
4. Luke and Mrs. Luke have stowed away.

Name _____

The Voyages of Dr. Dolittle
Part Three

GRAPHIC ORGANIZER

Problem Solving

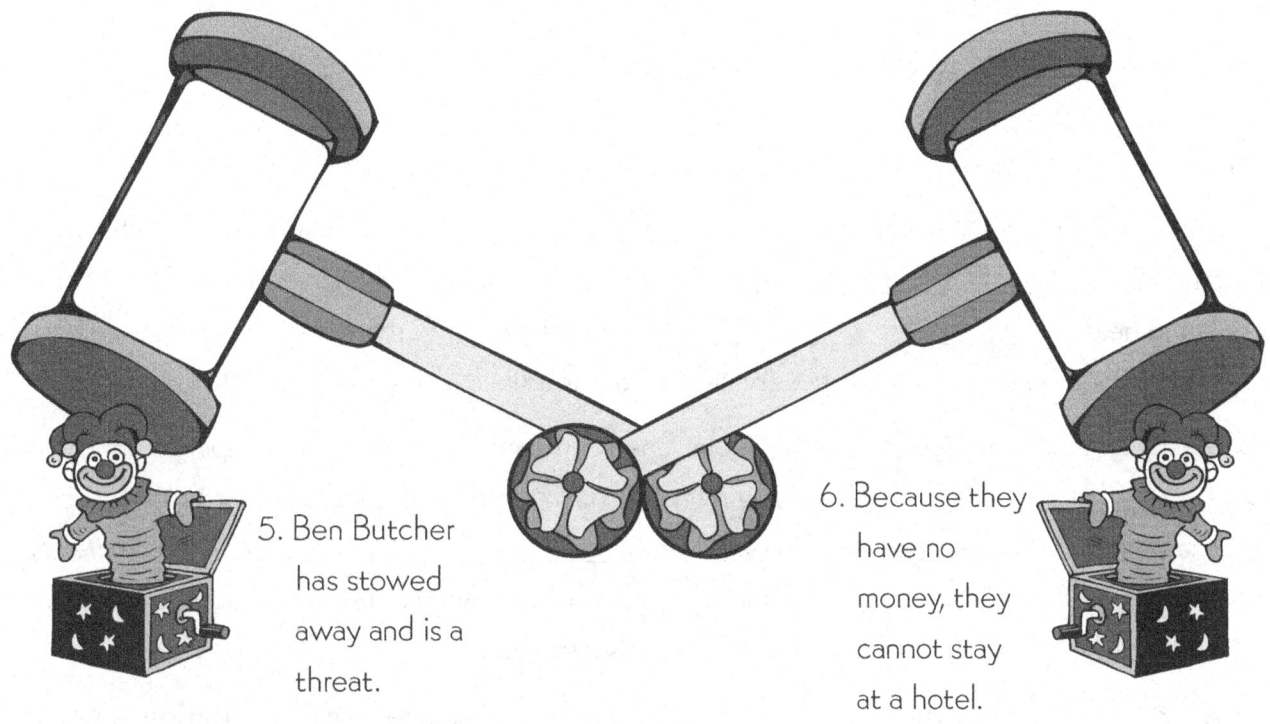

5. Ben Butcher has stowed away and is a threat.

6. Because they have no money, they cannot stay at a hotel.

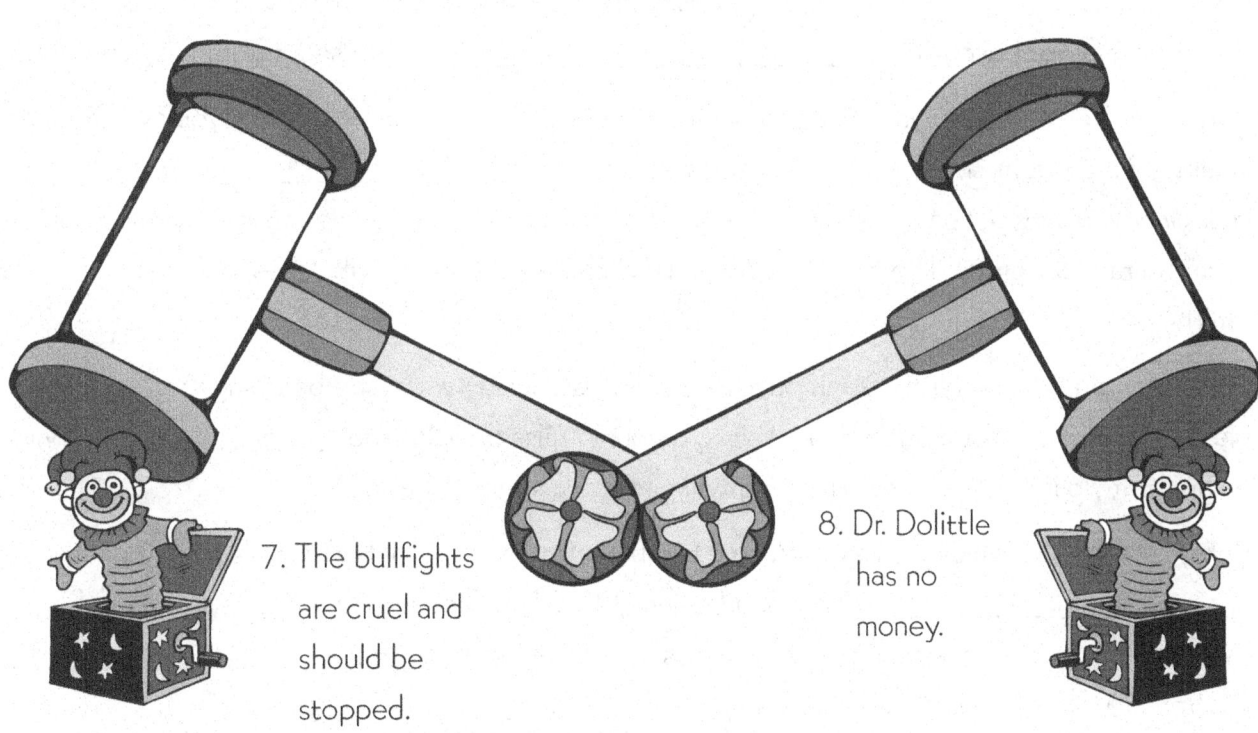

7. The bullfights are cruel and should be stopped.

8. Dr. Dolittle has no money.

The Novel ~ (Textbook p. 528)

The Voyages of Dr. Dolittle
Part Four

VOCABULARY
Activity 1

burrow	detected	fatigue	precipice	sulking
captivity	discourse	mystified	saturated	swooped
chortling	dismal	peak	stunned	wretched

1. Betsy heard the news. She was _____ (shocked). She felt as if she were standing on a _____ (an abrupt, downward slope). Her friend, Diana Smith, was being held in _____ (imprisonment)! Perhaps she should not have been surprised. Everyone knew that the government of the Republic of Mizmor was unfair and cruel.

2. She wasn't sure how to approach the problem. She had heard about people's escaping from the prison by _____ (digging by tunneling in the ground) under the prison walls. But it was the middle of the rainy season. The soil was _____ (filled completely) with water. Would that make digging a tunnel more difficult? And could a helicopter _____ (plunge) down and rescue Diana?

3. What had the local officials _____ (discovered)? Often, they invented reasons for taking people away to the _____ (gloomy; particularly bad) cells. Betsy was _____ (puzzled). She decided to phone Grizmas Jolodny, Chief of the Mizmor State Police. If they _____ (conversed; talked), it might help.

4. "Grizmas," Betsy shouted into the phone. The connection was poor. "Why have you put Diana Smith in jail?" She thought she could hear Grizmas Jolodny _____ (laughing or chuckling with satisfaction) on the other end. "Miss Betsy," he said, "Someone is stealing vegetables from the farmers' crops. The sketches drawn from the testimony of witnesses look just like Diana Smith."

5. "How can you be so foolish? Diana Smith is a scientist. What would she be doing stealing vegetables?" Grizmas chuckled again. "Miss Betsy, catching Miss Smith is the _____ (highest point) of my career! You'll see. The King will give me a special citation."

6. Betsy moaned, "Grizmas, you are making a terrible mistake." Miss Betsy's words made him want to _____ (be moodily silent). Finally he spoke. "Miss Betsy, if you are finished, I have to take care of important police business." He hung up. Betsy was _____ (suffering). She was also suffering from _____ (exhaustion).

Name _____

**The Voyages of Dr. Dolittle
Part Four**

VOCABULARY

Activity 11

Find the Synonym

Each vocabulary word is followed by three words. Circle the synonym.

1.	burrow	hurry	worry	tunnel
2.	wretched	joyous	miserable	wrenching
3.	precipice	cliff	appreciate	precious
4.	chortle	hurdle	chant joyously	horticulture
5.	discourse	talk	golf course	discard
6.	mystified	mystery	puzzled	mist
7.	peak	speak	beak	high point
8.	captivity	imprisonment	captive	capture
9.	saturated	hardened	filled	empty
10.	sulking	following	moping	hulking
11.	detected	detective	showed	discovered
12.	swooped	fainted	dove	fell asleep
13.	dismal	gloomy	bright	malice
14.	fatigue	rest	sleeping	exhaustion
15.	stunned	really happy	shocked	stung

The Novel ~ (Textbook p. 556)

The Voyages of Dr. Dolittle
Part Four
MORE ABOUT THE STORY
Writing Activity

You are the Fidgit with whom Dr. Dolittle talked. Write a page in your journal about one day in the aquarium.

Name _____

**The Voyages of Dr. Dolittle
Part Four**

MORE ABOUT THE STORY

Writing Activity

The Novel ~ (Textbook p. 556)

The Voyages of Dr. Dolittle
Part Four

GRAPHIC ORGANIZER
Focus on Writing

Part Four of *The Voyages of Dr. Dolittle* is packed with adventure. Imagine that each of the following four characters were writing a letter home about one adventure: Dr. Dolittle, Tommy Stubbins, Bumpo Kahbooboo, and Polynesia. The style of each letter would be very different from the others.

In the exercise below, there are four "letters." At the top of each letter is the topic it covers. At the bottom is the signature of the letter's author. As you write the letter, consider the following:

a. What parts of the event would the writer focus on? (For example, Tommy might tell you about the food he ate, whereas Dr. Dolittle might describe the sounds the animal made.)

b. What type of English would the letter be written in?

c. To whom would the letter be addressed?

You may invent some details to make the letter interesting, but try to make the letter's style reflect the writer.

I Found a Fidget

_____
_____
_____
_____
_____
_____
_____
_____
_____
_____
_____
_____
_____
_____
_____

Fondly,
Dr. Dolittle

Name _____

**The Voyages of Dr. Dolittle
Part Four**

GRAPHIC ORGANIZER

Focus on Writing

The Terrible Storm at Sea

_____
_____
_____
_____
_____
_____
_____
_____
_____
_____
_____

*Fondly,
Bumpo*

We Meet the Red Indians

_____
_____
_____
_____
_____
_____
_____
_____
_____
_____
_____

*Fondly,
Polynesia*

We Search for Long Arrow

_____
_____
_____
_____
_____

*Fondly,
Tommy*

The Novel ~ (Textbook p. 556)

The Voyages of Dr. Dolittle
Part Five

VOCABULARY
Activity 1

| assaulted | nourishing | slivers | topple |
| hastily | perplexed | shiftless | turmoil |

1. My brother and his friends are convinced that they have a real treasure map. Of course, they approach their search very seriously. My Uncle Harry says that at least they are not _____ (lacking in ambition). Did I tell you? They have their clubhouse up in our attic, and are very secretive about their plans. If I walk upstairs to the third floor, they all scatter and hide behind the old furniture we have up there.

2. When this happens, they move very _____ (hurriedly). They act as though they are being _____ (attacked) by an enemy. To help them keep up their energy, my mother makes them very _____ (sustaining; promoting growth) snacks. It bothers and _____ (puzzles) me that she goes along with their big pretense.

3. Sometimes they boast that the attic is a dangerous place to be, to show how brave they are. That's because Eric, my brother's friend, got a very little _____ (splinter) of wood in his finger one day up there.

4. All I know is that they make a mess in the attic. One time, there were the sounds of great _____ (an extremely disturbed state or condition): a crash and then some screams. It was one of their mock battles, and they had _____ (caused to fall; tumbled) an antique, very large bookcase, because they imagined that it was the wall of a fort. Well, you know what they say: *Boys will be boys!*

The Novel ~ (Textbook p. 584)

Name _____

**The Voyages of Dr. Dolittle
Part Five**

VOCABULARY

Activity II

Word Analogies

1. *build* is to *construct*, as **topple** is to
   a. knock over   b. keep standing   c. break in pieces
   Clue: Synonyms

2. *giving* is to *taking*, as **shiftless** is to
   a. hardworking   b. lazy   c. shifted
   Clue: Opposites

3. *befriend* is to *someone you'd like to get to know*, as **assault** is to
   a. friend   b. attack   c. enemy
   Clue: How you behave towards people in a particular role

4. *crevice* is to *crack*, as **hastily** is to
   a. quickly   b. slowly   c. hungrily
   Clue: Synonyms

5. *nourishing* is to *flourishing*, as **slivers** is to
   a. shivers   b. splinters   c. wood
   Clue: Rhyming

6. *meal* is to *cook*, as **turmoil** is to
   a. a cat   b. a dog   c. rioters in the streets
   Clue: Effect and cause

7. *permission* is to *commission*, as **perplex** is to
   a. puzzle   b. complex   c. complexion
   Clue: Prefixes *pre* and *com* + root word

The Novel ~ (Textbook p. 584)

The Voyages of Dr. Dolittle
Part Five

MORE ABOUT THE STORY
Writing Activity

> The title of your folktale is "How the Ragged-Eared Bagjagderags Came to Be Ragged-Eared." Begin your folktale with the words, "Once upon a time..." For information, consult Part Five, Chapters 5-10.

Name _____

**The Voyages of Dr. Dolittle
Part Five**
MORE ABOUT THE STORY
Writing Activity

The Novel ~ (Textbook p. 584)

The Voyages of Dr. Dolittle
Part Five

GRAPHIC ORGANIZER
Problem Solving

Many of the conflicts and problems in Dr. Dolittle's life are solved by animals. A war is won with the help of parrots, an island is moved by whales, and a lost Indian is found with the help of a beetle. Just imagine how many of today's problems could be solved if we could communicate with animals and get their help.

In the exercise below, six "headlines" tell of imaginary problems somewhere in the world. On the lines below each "article," explain how you would solve the problem using the help of animals, birds, fish, or insects.

New York City Garbage Crisis
New York City has too much garbage! The city is running out of space for garbage dumps, running short on trucks to remove the garbage, and running low on manpower to collect the garbage.

_____
_____
_____
_____
_____
_____

Computers Down Across the Country
For as yet undiscovered reasons, computers across the country have gone blank. The president has an urgent message that must get to the prime minister of England, but it is top secret. He is searching for a way to convey this message without compromising national security.

_____
_____
_____
_____
_____
_____
_____

Name _____

**The Voyages of Dr. Dolittle
Part Five**

GRAPHIC ORGANIZER

Problem Solving

Ship Hits Iceberg in Transatlantic Crossing
A ship hit an iceberg and is slowly sinking. Hundreds of people on board need rescuing, but other ships cannot get through the stormy weather to save them.

_____
_____
_____
_____
_____
_____
_____
_____
_____

L.A. in Fog of Smog
The windows of the high-rise buildings in Los Angeles are so covered with smog that the office workers can no longer see out of them. The windows desperately need a good cleaning, but there are far too few window washers to clean all those windows any time soon.

_____
_____
_____
_____
_____
_____
_____

Motorists Stranded on I-77
A snowstorm has hit. All down Interstate 77 motorists are stranded in the blinding snow. They need to be guided off the highway, but the snowplows can't get through and the traffic helicopters can't fly in the storm.

_____
_____
_____
_____
_____
_____
_____
_____

Drought Intensifies in Midwest
The summer has been unbearably dry and hot. The crops all across the Midwest are dying for lack of water and too much sun.

_____
_____
_____
_____
_____
_____
_____
_____
_____

The Novel ~ (Textbook p. 584)

The Voyages of Dr. Dolittle
Part Six
VOCABULARY — Activity 1

dignified	incognito	mortally	preposterous
embers	inquisitive	pondered	stealthily
endurance	jerkily	prolonged	

1. The Queen of Hearts is very _____ (noble), but she often travels _____ (with her identity concealed), so that no one will know who she is. She dresses as a washerwoman at these times. She wants privacy. She says that too many people are _____ (inclined to ask questions; curious), if she reveals her identity. Of course, sometimes people ask her to do their laundry—which is the job of a true washerwoman—which her servants think is absolutely _____ (absurd). The Queen has some odd notions, and sometimes she *does* hire herself out as a laundress.

3. Her serving girl told us about this one night, as we sat in front of the fireplace with the _____ (glowing fragments from a fire) just barely glowing. We all _____ (reflected on; thought about) this as we ate our popcorn and sizzling marshmallows.

4. One time, when the Queen was traveling in her coach, the horses started to neigh and move _____ (moving along marked by fits and starts). The coachmen were _____ (in a deadly or fatal manner; to an extreme degree) afraid. A highway robber had thrown rocks at them from the woods. Then he moved _____ (slowly; secretly; intended to escape observation) out of the woods.

5. The Queen was not afraid. But she does not like _____ (lengthened in time; extended) surprises. She stepped down from the carriage, dressed like a washerwoman, and said, "Young man. I have much to do! And I do not have the _____ (ability to sustain long, stressful events) for such a delay. What is it that you want?" "Madam," he asked. "Would you be willing to wash my clothes?" "Begone, young thief!" she cried. "You are as foolish as you are ignorant!" And the highwayman ran back into the woods. We all cheered the Queen's great courage.

The Novel ~ (Textbook p. 614)

Name _____

**The Voyages of Dr. Dolittle
Part Six**

VOCABULARY

Activity II

Word Analogies

1. *think about* is to **ponder**, as **incognito** is to
   a. be a cog in a wheel   b. be disguised   c. be uncovered
   Clue: Synonyms

2. *noble* is to *nobility*, as **dignified** is to
   a. dignity   b. digging a hole   c. nifty
   Clue: Adjective/noun

3. *scraps left over* are to *a meal*, as **embers** are to
   a. members   b. a wood or coal fire   c. ashes
   Clue: What remains at the conclusion of a particular activity?

4. *crevice* is to *crack*, as **mortally** is to
   a. mortuary   b. mortal   c. fatally
   Clue: Synonyms

5. *sad* is to *happy*, as **inquisitive** is to
   a. questioning   b. quiz   c. not curious
   Clue: Opposites

6. *insurance* is to *insure*, as **endurance** is to
   a. endure   b. persistence   c. not persisting
   Clue: Noun/verb

7. *stealthily* is to *openly*, as **jerkily** is to
   a. smoothly   b. jokingly   c. suddenly
   Clue: Opposites

8. *learned* is to *knowledgeable*, as **preposterous** is to
   a. posture   b. poster   c. ridiculous
   Clue: Synonyms

9. *propose* is to *pose*, as **prolong** is to
   a. extend   b. song   c. long
   Clue: Prefix *pro* dropped from root word

The Novel ~ (Textbook p. 614)   247

The Voyages of Dr. Dolittle
Part Six
MORE ABOUT THE STORY
Writing Activity

> You are the Court Poet in the court of King Jong. Add a stanza to those that appear on pages 617-618.

Name _____

**The Voyages of Dr. Dolittle
Part Six**

MORE ABOUT THE STORY

Writing Activity

The Novel ~ (Textbook p. 614)

The Voyages of Dr. Dolittle
Part Six

GRAPHIC ORGANIZER
Analyzing Character

Why is *The Voyages of Dr. Dolittle* beloved by so many readers? There are many answers. The talking animals, the fantastic adventures, the humor and language are some reasons. But one reason comes to mind before all the others: the character of Dr. Dolittle. Dr. Dolittle is the ideal friend, teacher, and parent. He makes us feel warm, secure, and wanted. Outside of tidiness, he has almost every good quality a person could want in a friend. In Part Six, more than in any other part of the book, Dr. Dolittle's good qualities are revealed in actions, dialogue, and narrative.

In the exercise below, eleven quotes from the story have been selected. On the line below each quote, write the character trait(s) that is reflected in the quote. On the lines provided at the end of the exercise, using the traits you have mentioned in the exercise, write a paragraph describing the character of Dr. Dolittle.

1. From the moment that he got up, early in the morning, till the time he went to bed, late at night—seven days a week—John Dolittle was busy, busy, busy.
   _____

2. In building this town the Doctor gave the Indians a lot of new ideas.
   _____

3. One of the first things that John Dolittle did was to search the mountains till he found iron and copper mines.
   _____

4. Then he set to work to teach the Indians how these metals could be melted and made into knives and plows...
   _____

5. In his kingdom the Doctor tried his hardest to do away with most of the old-fashioned pomp and grandeur of a royal court.
   _____

6. Then in the afternoon he taught school.
   _____

7. "These people have come to rely on me for a great number of things...I cannot close my eyes to what might happen if I should leave these people and run away."
   _____

8. "And no man wants to do unfair things to them who trust him..."
   _____

9. "Some day I must get all these things [the medicines discovered by Long Arrow] to England."
   _____

The Novel ~ (Textbook p. 614)

Name _____

**The Voyages of Dr. Dolittle
Part Six**

GRAPHIC ORGANIZER
Analyzing Character

10. One sight of the snail changed the Doctor completely. His eyes just sparkled with delight.

11. "I would like to do my best to cure his [the snail's] tail for him. It's the least I can do. After all, it was my fault, indirectly, that he got hurt."

The Character of Dr. Dolittle

_____
_____
_____
_____
_____
_____
_____
_____
_____
_____
_____
_____
_____
_____
_____

The Novel ~ (Textbook p. 614)

Glossary

A

abruptly (uh BRUPT lee) *adv.*: change without preparation or warning; unexpectedly

accumulated (uh KYOOM yoo layt id) *v.*: gathered or piled up little by little; amassed

acrid (AK rid) *adj.*: bitter

adroitly (uh DROYT lee) *adv.*: expertly

ailerons (A ler onz) *n.*: movable surfaces near the trailing edges of aircraft wings, used for banking

alley (AL lee) *n.*: a path in a park or garden

aloof (uh LOOF) *adj.*: reserved, withdrawn

anchorage (AING ker ij) *n.*: something that serves to hold a person or object firmly and securely

animosity (AN ih MAHS ih tee) *n.*: ill will; dislike

annoyance (uh NOY intz) *n.*: a source of irritation

antics (AN tiks) *n.*: attention-drawing, often wildly playful or funny acts or actions

anxious (ANK shuss) *adj.*: *here*, eager; *generally*, extremely worried and uneasy

apprehensive (APP re HEN siv) *adj.*: uneasy; concerned; viewing the future with anxiety or alarm

arid (AIR id) *adj.*: excessively dry

armadillo (ARM uh DILL oh) *n.*: a small insect-eating mammal with an armor-like shell

articulating (AR tick yoo LAYT ing) *v.*: pronouncing clearly

assaulted (us SALT id) *v.*: attacked violently

assented (uh SENT id) *v.*: agreed

attaché (AT uh SHAY) *n.*: a person who is on the staff of an ambassador or diplomat

augmented (awg MEN tid) *v.*: expanded; enlarged

awe (AW) *n.*: overwhelming feeling of admiration, fear, or wonder

B

bank (BAINK) *n.*: a controlled tilt made by a turning plane

barren (BAHR in) *adj.*: not bearing fruit or seed; desolate

battered (BAT terd) *adj.*: worn or damaged by hard usage or by blows

bellowed (BELL ode) *v.*: roared like a bull; cried out in a deep, blaring voice

benevolent (ben EV uh lint) *adj.*: kind and generous; inclined to doing good

berated (bee RAYT id) *v.*: scolded; expressed sharp, stern disapproval of

biased (BY ust) *adj.*: prejudiced

bigots (BIG its) *n.*: people who treat other people or groups of people with prejudice and intolerance

bland (BLAND) *adj.*: mild; expressionless

breed (BREED) *n.*: lineage; stock; strain; sort; kind; group

briers (BRY ers) *n.*: thorns; thistles

brutal (BROO til) *adj.*: cruel, harsh

bulged (BUHLJD) *v.*: swelled outward

burrow (BURR oh) *v.*: digging by tunneling in the ground

C

camouflaged (KAM ih flahjd) *v.*: concealed by means of disguise

canine (KAY nyn) *n.*: dog

captivity (kap TIV ih tee) *n.*: confinement; imprisonment; the state of being held captive

carp (KARP) *n.*: large freshwater fish

Glossary

cataract (KAT UH RAKT) *n.*: a condition of the eye in which the lens becomes cloudy and vision is impaired

cauterizing (KAUT er IYZ ing) *v.*: burning, with a hot iron

cautiously (KAW shis lee) *adv.*: behaving carefully because of fear of danger

chaos (KAY ahss) *n.*: a state of utter confusion

chattered (CHAT urd) *v.*: uttered rapidly repeated, unclear sounds

chivalrous (SHIV ihl rihs) *adj.*: gallant; courteous

chortling (CHORT ling) *v.*: uttering a chuckling laugh

clouted (CLOW tid) *v.*: struck forcefully, especially with the hand or fist

clustered (KLUS terd) *v.*: gathered into a group or bunch

clutching (KLUCH ing) *v.*: holding tightly with the hands

cobbler (KAHB lur) *n.*: repairer or maker of shoes

colossal (kuh LAHS il) *adj.*: of very great size; gigantic

commenced (cum MENST) *v.*: began

conjectured (kun JEK cherd) *v.*: guessed

consented (kun SEN tid) *v.*: gave approval; agreed

consternation (KAHN ster NAY shin) *n.*: amazement or dismay that hinders or throws into confusion

contempt (kun TEMPT) *n.*: scorn

contraption (kun TRAP shin) *n.*: device; gadget

converse (kahn VERS) *v.*: exchange thoughts and opinions in speech; talk with

cordial (KOR jil) *adj.*: friendly and warm

corridor (KOR ih DOOR) *n.*: a long passageway or hallway in a building; often with doors opening to rooms off of it

covey (CUV ee) *n.*: a small group of game birds, especially partridges or quail

cowardly (COW urd lee) *adv.*: in a weak manner; not bravely

crevasse (kruh VASS) *n.*: a very deep and wide break or opening

cul-de-sac (KUL DUH SAK) *n.*: a passage or street that is closed at one end

cunningly (KUN ing lee) *adv.*: cleverly or craftily

currency (KER uhn see) *n.*: money

D

deflating (dee FLAYT ing) *v.*: releasing air or gas from

delineate (dih LIN ee ayt) *v.*: to describe with accuracy or in detail

demeanor (dih MEAN ur) *n.*: conduct, behavior; facial appearance

derelicts (DEHR uh LIKTS) *n.*: persons abandoned or forgotten

descent (dih SENT) *n.*: the act of proceeding from a higher place to a lower one

desolate (DEZ uh lit) *adj.*: empty; having no inhabitants or visitors

despise (dih SPYZ) *v.*: to regard with contempt

detected (dee TEK tid) *v.*: discovered or determined the existence or presence of

devoid (dih VOYD) *adj.*: empty; not the usual or expected

dignified (DIG nih fyd) *adj.*: noble; showing or expressing dignity; honored or esteemed

diminishing (dih MIN ish ing) *adj.*: decreasing; become gradually less

discourse (DISS korce) *v.*: converse; talk

dismal (DIZ mul) *adj.*: gloomy or depressing; particularly bad

Glossary

dismally (DIZ muh lee) *adv.*: threateningly; miserably

distinguish (diss TIN gwish) *v.*: to see as being separate or different; to recognize a difference in

dunes (DOONZ) *n.*: a sand hill or sand ridge formed by the wind, usually in desert regions or near the ocean

E

efficiency (eh FISH ihn see) *n.*: effectiveness; productivity

egotism (EE go TIZ um) *n.*: an exaggerated sense of self-importance

elation (ee LAY shun) *n.*: delight

emaciated (ih MAY shee AYT id) *adj.*: wasted away physically; malnourished

embers (EM burz) *n.*: glowing fragments from a fire

eminent (EM in ent) *adj.*: outstanding; prominent

emphatic (em FAT ik) *adj.*: definite; accented

endurance (in DUR intz) *n.*: the ability to sustain a prolonged stressful effort or activity

engineered (EN jin eared) *v.*: planned; designed or produced

epic (EH pick) *adj.*: heroic; extending beyond the usual in size or scope

excursions (ex CER zhuns) *n.*: brief, pleasure trips

F

fatigue (fih TEEG) *n.*: weariness or exhaustion from labor, exertion, or stress

filed (FY uhld) *v.*: marched in a line, one after the other

flinched (FLINCHT) *v.*: drew back or away, as if from something dangerous; winced

flushed (FLUSHT) *v.*: drove out of hiding

forage (FOR idge) *v.*: search for provisions or food

formidable (FOR mid ih bul) *adj.*: threatening; causing fear, dread, and apprehension

frenzied (FREN zeed) *adj.*: desperately agitated

freshet (FRESH IT) *n.*: a sudden rise in the level of a stream or a flooding caused by heavy rain or rapidly melting snow or ice

frowned (FROUND) *v.*: contracted the brow in displeasure; looked displeased

furiously (FYOOR ee us lee) *adv.*: a stormy or turbulent appearance

G

gabardine (GAB er DEEN) *n.*: a durable fabric used in making suits and dresses

gait (GAYT) *n.*: a manner of walking, stepping, or running

galvanized (GAL vuh nyzd) *v.*: plated with zinc to resist rust; motivated

gamboling (GAM buh ling) *v.*: skipping, dancing, frolicking

gash (GASH) *n.*: cut or wound

gasp (GASP) *v.*: to catch one's breath with shock

gazelles (guh ZELZ) *n.*: small, graceful African antelopes

gesturing (JEST cher ing) *v.*: motioning with the body or the limbs to express an idea, a feeling, or an attitude

glacier (GLAY sher) *n.*: a large mass of ice and snow

gleaned (GLEEND) *v.*: gathered information bit by bit

gradually (GRAJ oo lee) *adv.*: slowly

gravely (GRAYV lee) *adv.*: with serious bearing or manner

Glossary

H

hamper (HAM pur) *v.*: interfere with; restrict the movement of

hastily (HAYS tih lee) *adv.*: rapidly and often with little attention to detail; hurriedly

heaps (HEEPS) *n.*: piles

hillocks (HILL ahks) *n.*: small hills

hitch (HICH) *v.*: tie; to fasten

horizon (hor I zun) *n.*: a line or circle that forms the apparent boundary between earth and sky

hospitable (hahs PIT uh bul) *adj.*: giving a generous and friendly welcome

hurl (HERL) *v.*: throw forcefully; fling

I

imbecile (IM buh sil) *n.*: a simple-minded person

immobility (IM oh BILL ih tee) *n.*: the state of being motionless

impatiently (im PAYSH int lee) *adv.*: restlessly; in a manner that is without patience

impertinent (im PUR tih nint) *adj.*: rude

implored (im PLORD) *v.*: begged; asked for earnestly

impudence (IMP you duntz) *n.*: bold and shameless rudeness

incessantly (in SESS int lee) *adv.*: in an unceasing manner; without intermission; continually

incognito (IN kahg NEE toe) *adj.*: with one's identity concealed

incomprehensible (IN com pree HEN sih bul) *adj.*: not possible to understand

indefinitely (in DEF in it lee) *adv.*: having no fixed or specific limit

inevitable (in EV it uh bul) *adj.*: unavoidable

inexorable (in EX ser uh bul) *adj.*: unyielding; relentless

inflammatory rheumatism (in FLAM uh TOR ee ROOM uh TIZ im) *n.*: a disease characterized by painful swelling and stiffness in the joints or muscles

inherent (in HIR int) *adj.*: inborn

innovations (IN oh VAY shunz) *n.*: new ideas, methods, or devices

inoculation (in OCK you LAY shun) *n.*: vaccination

inquisitive (in KWIZ ih tiv) *adj.*: inclined to ask questions; curious

interplanetary (IN ter PLAN uh tehr ee) *adj.*: occuring between planets or between planets and the sun

irritable (EAR it uh bul) *adj.*: cranky; upset and impatient

J

jagged (JAG id) *adj.*: raggedly notched; sharply irregular on the surface or borders

jerked (JURKT) *v.*: pushed, pulled, or twisted suddenly

jerkily (JURK ih lee) *adv.*: moving along marked by fits and starts

juncture (JUNK cher) *n.*: point of time

jutting (JUT ting) *v.*: projecting outward

K

keener (KEEN er) *adj.*: quicker; sharper

L

lariat (LAIR ee ut) *n.*: a long rope that is used with a noose to catch livestock

laths (LATHZ) *n.*: thin, narrow strips of wood used to make a backing for plaster or stucco

Glossary

launching (LAWN ching) *n.*: to send forth with force; to release

limber (LIM ber) *v.*: make flexible; loosen up

limply (LIMP lee) *adv.*: lacking in strength, vigor, or firmness

lingered (LING urd) *v.*: was slow in parting from

loam (LOAM) *n.*: fertile soil consisting of clay, silt, and sand

M

majestic (muh JES tuk) *adj.*: regal; grand

maneuvered (mun OOV erd) *v.*: to manage or move into or out of a position

marina (muh REEN uh) *n.*: landing pier for docking small boats

martial (MAR shuhl) *adj.*: warlike; military

Mayday (MAY DAY) *n.*: an international radiotelephone distress signal used by ships and aircraft

melancholy (MEL in KAHL ee) *n.*: a feeling of sadness

mellow (MEL oh) *adj.*: made gentle by age or experience; pleasant, agreeable, laid-back

metamorphosis (MET uh mor FO siss) *n.*: a profound change

meticulously (meh TICK you lus lee) *adv.*: extremely careful in the treatment of details

microbes (MY krohbz) *n.*: very small disease-causing bacteria or organisms

miscellaneous (miss uh LAY nee us) *adj.*: consisting of various things, traits, or members

monitoring (MAHN ih ter ing) *v.*: watching, keeping track of, or checking

mortally (MORT uh lee) *adv.*: in a deadly or fatal manner; to an extreme degree

mourning (MORN ing) *n.*: the state of grieving over a death

mutely (MYOOT lee) *adv.*: silently

mystified (MISS tih FYD) *adj.*: puzzled; perplexed

N

naturalist (NAT chur uh list) *n.*: one who studies natural science

nonplused (nahn PLUST) *v.*: puzzled; unsure; at a loss of what to say, think, or do

notion (NO shun) *n.*: idea

nourishing (NUR ish ing) *adj.*: nutritious; promoting growth; sustaining

O

obliging (uh BLY jing) *adj.*: ready to do favors

obscure (ub SKYOOR) *adj.*: remote and secluded; not prominent or famous

obstinate (AHB stin it) *adj.*: stubborn

ominous (AHM in us) *adj.*: threatening; foreshadows evil or disaster

ordeal (oar dee UHL) *n.*: a severe trial or experience

P

pace (PAIS) *n.*: the rate of movement in stepping and walking

pathetic (puh THET ik) *adj.*: extremely pitiful; bringing to mind pity, sympathy, or sorrow

pathos (PATH ose) *n.*: feelings of pity

peak (PEEK) *n.*: the top of a mountain or hill; highest point

pedestal (PED ih stuhl) *n.*: the base of an upright structure

peeved (PEEVED) *adj.*: annoyed

pension (PEN SHUN) *n.*: a payment received periodically by a retired person

perched (PERCHT) *v.*: to settle or rest on a usually high place

perilous (PEHR ih lus) *adj.*: dangerous

perished (PEHR isht) *v.*: ceased to exist; died

perplexed (pur PLEXT) *adj.*: filled with doubt, uncertainty, or confusion; puzzled

persistently (per SIS tint lee) *adv.*: continuing without change; relentlessly; stubbornly

pestilence (PES tih lintz) *n.*: a natural population suddenly and greatly enlarged; epidemic

philosopher (fil AHSS uh fer) *n.*: one who studies ideas and seeks wisdom

phobia (FO bee yuh) *n.*: an exaggerated, illogical fear

phosphorescent (FAHS fer ESS int) *adj.*: glowing that is caused by the absorption of light

pippins (PIP inz) *n.*: a variety of apple

pliant (PLY uhnt) *adj.*: easily bent; flexible

ploy (PLOY) *n.*: a playful game; a plan or tactic that is different from ordinary contact

poised (POYZD) *v.*: balanced

pondered (PAHN durd) *v.*: contemplated; thought; reflected on

portable (POR tih bul) *adj.*: capable of being carried or moved about

precipice (PREH sih PEECE) *n.*: an abrupt, downward slope

premium (PREE mee um) *n.*: an extra amount charged in addition to the usual price

preposterous (prih PAHS tur us) *adj.*: contrary to nature, reason, or common sense; absurd

prerogative (prih RAHG ih tiv) *n.*: an exclusive or special right, power, or privilege; option

procession (pro SESH un) *n.*: a group of individuals moving along in an orderly way

prodigious (prah DIDJ iss) *adj.*: immense; extraordinary size

profusion (pro FEW zhun) *n.*: a great supply; superabundance

prolonged (PRO longd) *adj.*: lengthened in extent, scope, or range; extended

prominent (PRAHM in int) *adj.*: widely and popularly known; standing out

prone (PROAN) *adj.*: lying face down

provisions (pruh VIZH unz) *n.*: a stock of needed materials and supplies

prowling (PROW ling) *v.*: to move about in a slow, secret way, intended to escape observation

pruning (PROON ing) *v.*: trimming; cutting back

pummeled (PUM meld) *v.*: thump and pound; to strike repeatedly

punctured (PUNK churd) *v.*: pierced with a pointed instrument or object

purgative (PUR guh tiv) *n.*: a medicine that cleanses the intestines

R

racket (RAK it) *n.*: confused, loud noise

radiant (RAY dee int) *adj.*: shining; marked by an expression of love, confidence, or happiness

rafters (RAFT erz) *n.*: beams of a ceiling

ratified (RAD ih fyd) *v.*: approved; upheld

rattle (RAT il) *v.*: to make or cause a rapid succession of short, sharp noises; clatter

reconnoiter (REE cun oy ter) *v.*: to make an exploratory or preliminary survey, inspection, or examination

Glossary

reflecting (rih FLECKT ing) *v.*: thinking about calmly or quietly

refraction (ree FRAK shun) *n.*: the bending of a ray of light as it passes from the air through water or glass

refuge (REF yooj) *n.*: a safe haven or sanctuary; a place of shelter

register (REJ ih stur) *n.*: a written record containing regular entries of items, details, events, or names

resented (ree ZEN tid) *v.*: felt annoyed with

resilient (ree ZIL yint) *adj.*: flexible and elastic; able to return to its original shape after being pressed out of shape by some force

revelation (REV ih lay shun) *n.*: the discovery of something previously unknown; something unexpected that creates surprise

roan (ROAN) *n.*: a brownish-red colored horse

rupees (ROO peez) *n.*: Indian currency; at the time of the story, one rupee was worth about ten cents

S

saturated (SACH ur AYT id) *v.*: filled completely

savoring (SAY vohr ing) *v.*: relishing; enjoying

scattered (SKAT erd) *v.*: to separate and go in various directions

scrambled (SKRAM buld) *v.*: hurried; climbed up by moving quickly

seasoned (SEE zuhnd) *adj.*: experienced

sedative (SED uh TIV) *adj.*: tending to calm or soothe

sentimental (SENT im EN tul) *adj.*: having or showing tender feelings

sequestered (sih KWES terd) *v.*: secluded; set off; set apart

shaft (SHAFT) *n.*: beam or beacon of light; a sharply defined beam that shines through an opening

sheen (SHEEN) *n.*: luster; glimmer

shiftless (SHIFT liss) *adj.*: marked by a lack of ambition, energy, or purpose; lazy

simultaneous (sy mul TAY nee us) *adj.*: occurring at the same time

sinews (SIN yooz) *n.*: tendons that connect the muscles with other parts of the body; tendons that have been dressed for use as cords or thread

skeptics (SKEHP ticks) *n.*: doubters

sketch (SKECH) *n.*: a rough drawing

slithered (SLITH erd) *v.*: moved or walked with a sliding motion, as a snake; slid unsteadily down a surface, from side to side

slivers (SLIV urz) *n.*: long, slender pieces cut off of larger pieces; splinters

solace (SAHL uss) *n.*: comfort

solemn (SAHL um) *adj.*: serious, grave

solitary (SAHL ih TAIR ee) *adj.*: being, living, or going alone or without companions

sorghum molasses (SORE gum muh LASS iss) *n.*: sweet syrup made from the juicy stalks of a cereal grass

specimen (SPESS ih men) *n.*: a portion of material for use in testing, examination, or study; a sample

spectators (SPEK tay ters) *n.*: one who looks or watches

spore (SPOR) *n.*: a simple one-celled organism produced by plants, fungi, and other microorganisms

staggering (STAG er ing) *v.*: having difficulty standing; reeling from side to side

Glossary

stalk (STAWK) *v.*: walk in a slow, stiff manner

stalwart (STAHL wert) *adj.*: marked by outstanding strength and vigor of body, mind, or spirit

stealthily (STEL thih lee) *adv.*: secretly; in a sneaky manner

stern (STURN) *adj.*: strict; forbidding

strep (STREP) *n.*: an abbreviation of streptococcus, a disease-causing bacteria

stunned (STUND) *adj.*: made senseless or dizzy as if by a blow; shocked

sturdy (STER dee) *adj.*: firmly built and strong; hardy

sufficient (suh FISH int) *adj.*: enough to meet the needs of a situation

sulking (SUL king) *v.*: being moodily silent

superfluous (suh PER flew uss) *adj.*: being more than is sufficient; unnecessary; needless

superior (suh PEER ee ur) *adj.*: of higher grade or quality; greater in quality, amount

surgeon (SUR jun) *n.*: a medical specialist who performs surgery

surplus (SIR plus) *n.*: superabundance

suspending (sus PEN ding) *v.*: hanging from above

swagger (SWAG er) *n.*: a walk with an air of overbearing self-confidence

swathed (SWAWTHD) *v.*: wrapped

swell (SWELL) *n.*: a long often huge wave or waves coming one after the other

swindle (SWIN dul) *n.*: an act of deceit; a trick

swooped (SWOOPT) *v.*: plunged suddenly; moved in a sweeping arc

synchronize (SIN kruh NYZ) *v.*: to set to the same time, as with watches; to operate, move, or work, at the same rate and exactly together

T

tarpaulin (TAR pihl in) *n.*: a piece of waterproof material used for protecting exposed objects or areas

taut (TAWT) *adj.*: tense; tightly stretched

teeming (TEEM ing) *v.*: swarming, as with people or animals; falling in torrents, as with rain

tenacity (tih NASS ih tee) *n.*: perseverance; persistence in seeking something valued or desired

tiresome (TYRE sum) *adj.*: possessing a quality that tires, bores, or annoys

topple (TAHP il) *v.*: to fall or tumble from top-heaviness

tragically (TRAJ ick lee) *adv.*: sadly; having a disastrous conclusion; regrettably

translucent (tranz LOO sint) *adj.*: allowing light to pass through

turmoil (TUR moy il) *n.*: an extremely disturbed state or condition

U

uncanny (un CAN ee) *adj.*: mysterious; weird

uncomprehendingly (un CAHM pre HEND ing lee) *adv.*: without understanding

undercurrent (UN der KUHR int) *n.*: a force which is not readily visible

uniform (YOO nih form) *adj.*: having the same form; alike

V

vague (VAIG) *adj.*: unclear

valiant (VAL yint) *adj.*: brave

vanished (VAN isht) *v.*: passed quickly from sight; disappeared

Glossary

vapor (VAY per) *adj.*: steam

varnished (VAR nisht) *v.*: coated with varnish; gave a glossy appearance to

venturesome (VEN chur SUM) *adj.*: adventurous

veranda (ver AND uh) *n.*: an open porch extending along one or more sides of a building, at the ground level

vibrations (vy BRAY shins) *n.*: shaking to and fro movements; a quivering or trembling motion

vicinity (vih SIN ih tee) *n.*: a surrounding area or district; neighborhood

virtually (VER choo uh lee) *adv.*: almost entirely; nearly; for all practical purposes

vitality (vy TAL ih tee) *n.*: full of energy, strength, and vigor

voyages (VOY ij iz) *n.*: act or instances of traveling; journeys by water

vulnerable (VUL nur uh bul) *adj.*: capable of being physically or emotionally wounded

W

wistfully (WHIST fuh lee) *adv.*: showing longings; wishfully

wonderment (WUN der mint) *n.*: amazement

wretched (RECH id) *adj.*: appearing mean or miserable; suffering

writhes (RYTHES) *v.*: twists and turns, as in pain